AF540635

Adult Education

DPH Education Series

ADULT EDUCATION

U K SINGH • K N SUDARSHAN

DISCOVERY PUBLISHING HOUSE PVT. LTD.
NEW DELHI-110 002

First Published - 1996
Reprinted - 2017

ISBN: 978-81-7141-335-5

Adult Education

Published by:
DISCOVERY PUBLISHING HOUSE PVT. LTD.
4383/4B, Ansari Road, Darya Ganj
New Delhi-110 002 (India)
Phone: +91-11-23279245, 23253475, 43596065
E-mail: discoverypublishinghouse@gmail.com
sales@discoverypublishinggroup.com
web: www.discoverypublishinggroup.com

Printed at:
Infinity Imaging Systems
Delhi

Preface

The *DPH Education Handbook* has been created to provide access to information about contemporary topics in education. Practitioners and students at all levels in education have a need to know what is happening today, in addition to historical treatments within the literature.

Each chapter within the Handbook is designed to provide the user with needed "state-of-the-art" information as well as further sources of information. One of the significant features of each chapter is the inclusion of specific programmes, projects and activities so that the researcher can locate human resources as well as the literature.

The handbook will be of use to graduate and post graduate students in education and to practicing teachers, administrators, librarians and planners. The chapters and the further sources of information cited in each book should lead the reader to thousands of people and documents for either research or programme planning purposes.

An effort to achieve universal and effective education is based on a recognition of the rights of students to basic education that enables them to thrive in a complex society, as well as a realization the technological and economic growth is facilitated by increasing the numbers of students, even those with poor academic progresses, who are, in fact successful in learning. Thus, recent and current efforts improve education serve both private and social interests.

This series is addressed to administrators, planners and educators working in the field of education and training with a view to stimulating interest and attention in the areas of education and its related fields. It is also addressed to a growing number of teachers and instructors who will be practitioners in education and who will need to be acquainted with the modern aspects of educational practice and development. Many ideas, generalisations and discussions presented in this series should also prove useful to employing organisations committed to provide training facilities within their establishments—leading to effective mutual participation by institutions and organisations.

The editors wishes to thank the contributors, as well as those organizations that gave permission to publish their extracts, chapters etc.

Editors

Contents

1 Current Crisis in Adult Education

Nowadays most of us are all too familiar with dire warnings about existing or impending crises that would otherwise often escape our notice as we tackle personal challenges and the problems of day-to-day living. We are entitled, and probably well advised, to treat overriding assertions about the critical condition of this or that aspect of human experience with a dose of scepticism. So it is only after careful forethought that the spectre of adult education in crisis is raised at the outset to prepare the way for an understanding of adult education as vocation. The dimensions of the present crisis addressed in this chapter do, however, serve as a necessary prelude to describing prospects for a relevant and emancipatory practice of adult education. These call for a critically informed, transformative pedagogy.

In what ways can we say that the field of endeavour called adult education is in crisis? We can refer initially to the difficulties adult educators have always come up against in maintaining a firm, minimally financed, institutional basis from which to practise their vocation. These difficulties are apparent even within institutions, such as community colleges, where the mandate is, supposedly, entirely given over to adult education. The struggle for a share of resources and legitimation is much more clear-cut for adult education components operating within larger institutional settings. And adult educators working in non-formal community settings, usually without benefit of sanction that comes from affiliation with larger institutions and government departments, are constantly confronted with the need to sustain a modest resource base.

The problems associated with marginal status persist for adult education practitioners even now that mounting public rhetoric is proclaiming the virtues and necessity of continuing education for adults under the rubric of lifelong learning. However, widespread enthusiasm for the notion of lifelong learning in recent years seems to have presented the opportunity for adult education to move from its marginal role in society towards centre stage and, understandably, adult educators have wanted to sieze upon the opportunity. Unfortunately, there is a real danger of adult educators becoming so pleased to be recognized that they will find themselves lending support to the subversion of voluntary lifelong learning in favour of mandatory lifelong schooling. If at this juncture such a prospect seems a little far-fetched, it is evident that an eagerness to consolidate more substantial recognition for the role of adult education has been accompanied by a proclivity to incorporate within the field of practice an increasing array of pedagogical techniques, trappings of a cult of efficiency which harbour the germs of the current crisis in adult education.

While the cult of efficiency is most pronounced in North American adult education practice, the tendency is well untrenched elsewhere. In Britain and other western European countries, formal adult education practice has probably been, on the whole, better informed by philosophical writings and by more clear-cut commitments to social concerns. However, even in these countries, evidence of a clearer understanding of the issues at stake and a tradition of practical social commitment have not countered within adult education practice a growing, taken-for-granted fixation on technique.

Fixation on technique

The cult of efficiency refers to a growing, and seductive, tendency to make more and more areas of human endeavour amenable to measurement and technobureaucratic control according to what is invoked as a scientific approach. It elevates technical rationality to a position of undisputed pre-eminence over other forms of human thought and discourse. Although currently very expensive, this is not a new phenomenon. American public school administrators, for example, were extolling the virtues of scientific management principles, as applied in business and industry, in the early 1900s, and a resurgence of faith in the application of scientific principles to public school administration and curriculum development has coincided with each recurrence of general public demand for 'back to basics' and for greater accountability. Until recently, though, adult education, even in the United States, has not been quite so susceptible to the ideological demands of the cult of efficiency.

Why should we be alarmed at the prospect of adult education paying homage to the cult of efficiency after the manner of method-oriented pedagogues who have been able to direct, or misdirect, their techniques on to American public schools? After all, aren't efficiency and the application of technique at the core of prevailing political rhetoric on the need for educational initiatives to help us meet the technological revolution of 'post-industrial society' as we head towards the year 2000? The prospect becomes alarming when we witness aspects of the cult of efficiency intruding into more and more aspects of our everyday lives, as though determined to organize all human activities within scientific guidelines. And yet there is still a prevalent and sadly mistaken tendency in today's society for educators to regard technology as something neutral and to ignore the very subjective practical consequences that accompany its deployment. Even as this chapter is being written, the practical consequences of applying bio-medical techniques to provide surrogate mothers for child bearing are only just beginning to unravel.

On balance, it may well turn out that the creation of life via surrogate motherhood will enrich human experience, but it is clear that the deployment of technique in the case of 'test tube babies' has encroached upon a vital domain of this fundamental creative experience before we have been able to get to grips with its subjectively grounded practical consequences. The provision of surrogate motherhood via the deployment of bio-medical technique is but one of a legion of examples we can cull from contemporary society to confirm that technocratic values are taking precedence over practical (ethical) viewpoints in shaping vital areas of our everyday lives. Martin Heidegger captured the essence of the predicament and the challenge in the following passage:

> Modern technology too is a means to an end. That is why the instrumental conception of technology conditions every attempt to bring man into the right relation to technology. Everything depends on our manipulating technology in the proper manner as a means. We will, as we say,' 'Get' technology 'spiritually in hand'. We will master it. The will to mastery becomes all the more urgent the more technology threatens to slip from human control.

Though the trends and concerns noted in the preceding paragraphs are drawn from a North American context, the technicist obsession they portray can be readily characterized by similar examples in other countries. It is not only in the USA that modern adult education practice has so readily adopted the cult of efficiency. The extent to which adult education practice in Britain, for example, has fallen in with the government's ideologically driven skills training schemes is instructive, particularly in view of the somewhat greater inclination among British adult educators than their American counterparts towards social critique and political analysis.

Among defenders of the terrain encroached upon by inappropriately applied technical schemes is a fraternity of adult educators whose ranks dwindle as so many of their associates, wilfully or unwrittingly, have themselves joined in the endeavour to hoist the ideology of technical competence and technocratic professionalism to a position of undisputed prominence. In this book we will be referring to the works of some of these adult educators who recognize that the vital territory threatened by a cult of efficiency provides sustenance for men and women to exercise a significant degree of autonomy in their day-to-day lives with a minimum of interference and coercion from outside experts and officialdom. The presumption of a relatively autonomous domain, however meagre, in the everyday lives of men and women is surely a prerequisite for any notions of a real participatory democracy and genuine self-directed learning.

These concerns are not highlighted as part of a polemic against technological innovation. But they do represent a deep anxiety at the way so much of adult education has resorted to the ideology of technique in recent times to guide its practice. The growing tendency towards inappropriate applications of technical, mechanistic formats, which will be termed technicism throughout the course of this book, to steer adult education endeavours is what constitutes the current crisis. Such formats commend themselves to us because they convey an impression of being systematic: they impart a sense of certainty and order to educators and learners.

Adult learning situations managed by technical formulations, such as standardized pre-packaged curricula and preconceived needs assessment instruments put together by those who have contrived to become designated as experts tend towards artificiality and detachment from real life everyday experience. Formalized adult education is thus transformed into the technical planning of instruction and literally gets in the way of individual learners' ability to think critically, and to evaluate everyday experience on their own account. Independence, reflective, thought on the part of the individual learner is effectively usurped by the expert designers of technocratic curricula and those who embrace their technicist assumptions. With them at the helm, adult education as an organized system will serve to subvert critical powers of insight and imagination. They steer modern adult education practice away from any real prospects it might have of developing into a genuinely transformative pedagogy for a more just society.

We will deal further with the assumptions and consequences of adult education programmes based on technocratic models later in this chapter. It suffices to note at this point that adult learning situations managed by technical formulations, such as standardized pre-packaged curricula and preconceived needs assessment instruments put together by experts, become distortions—or at best, mere adumbrations—of our everyday experiences. Vital dimensions of these experiences, which cannot be adequately dealt with from the standpoint of a technocratic paradigm, refer us to practical and ethical activities of adulthood. These activities call for thoughtful, critical assessment and are not reducible, simplistically, to a finite series of preordained skills and competences.

The concerns laid out here are not new. Thoughtful adult educators have been troubled for some time by the uncritical acceptance within their field of practice of assumptions, techniques, and stipulations associated with the cult of efficiency. It is over half a century since the much cited American adult educator, Eduard C.Lindeman, wrote in The Meaning of Adult Education about the dangers of specialism and preoccupation with method. And three decades have passed since Richard Hoggart, an English adult educator, noted in his eminently readable book, The Uses of Literacy, that 'the problem is acute and pressing—how that freedom may be kept in any sense a meaningful thing whilst the processes of centralization and technological development continue'. Hoggart was particularly concerned about 'the division between the technical languages of the experts and the extraordinarily low level of the organs of mass communication'. Yet, despite the classic accounts of Hoggart and Lindeman, and the frequent reference by contemporary adult educators to these two books, the crisis has deepened since their times. The obsession with methodology and technique has become so embedded in adult education practice and research that many practitioners are no longer able to recognize the way it controls and shapes adult learning activities. It does nothing to offset the 'low level of the organs of mass communication'. If anything, a modern practice of adult education steered by technical rationality serves to reinforce the manipulative, controlling effects of popular mass communications rather than unmasking them.

The immediate challenge, evaded by most adult educators preoccupied with a plethora of strategies such as self-paced learning, computer-guided instruction, learning contracts, and competency-based education, lies in determining how to deploy methods and technology as subordinate, supporting optional functions that are not allowed to steer the adult education process. Unhappily, these media themselves are becoming the predominant message of modern adult education practice. An overall orientation characterizing adult education as a fundamentally technocratic endeavour, even in the way it informs us about learning how to learn, remains undisturbed by frequent references to the importance of critical thinking. Critical thinking in adult education, it seems, is either to be relativized so that it does not come into direct confrontation with the predominant ideologies, texts, and authorities of the field or it is reduced, with technocratic abandon, to a series of critical thinking 'skills' or 'competencies'. Either way, the critical edge is lost.

Although a few adult educators have continued to point out, and to resist, the more obvious aspects of the cult of efficiency, the crisis is deepening. Increasingly, an eagerness on the part of many adult educators to be accepted as socially relevant has become intertwined with a belief that most of the major ills of society, as well as individual learning deficiencies, can be ultimately solved by construing the underlying principles of the field in technocratic formats. So as adult educators lay on techniques in the form of learning contracts to direct adults on how to become self-directed learners, for example, we are co-opted by the cult of efficiency and technical rationality. An underlying principle of adult education practice that has to do with the central importance of the learner's past experience and a responsibility to preserve the integrity of voluntary participation is undermined when technique steers, and shapes, the educational process.

Techniques that shape the learning environment are built into a vast array of standardized, systematically designed, learning packages for adult students. Their prescriptive intent is discernible even when they are accompanied by such labels as 'self-directed', 'learner-dirven', and 'self paced'. The practice of applying significant value-laden terms to characterize technocratic curriculum formats is widespread. These are deployed quite promiscuously as a strategy to make extreme rationalization of the curriculum more enticing. And there is no doubt that adult educators are being seduced by exemplars of extreme rationalization such as competency-based learning, and the many skills-based curriculum formats which purport to teach us how to cope and how to live. The latter are proffered under the rubrics of 'coping skills', 'literacy skills', and 'life skills'. The climax of all this will come, presumably, with an immature, somewhat pathetic, faith in the notion that coping and living can be reduced to a definitive number of identifiable skills or competences.

In this context the idea of lifelong learning has become little more than a slogon. And,while slogans do have their usefulness, the term lifelong learning is used excessively as a label to legitimize all manner of adult education programmes. This usually precludes any need to make a critical appraisal of their technocratic and prescriptive content. Lifelong learning thus becomes lifelong training or lifelong schooling in line with technicist ideology. If anything, when deployed to legitimize prescriptive curriculum formats, it now signifies the erosion of the voluntary nature of adult education. It becomes the vehicle from which a technicist ideology further subverts the role of the adult educator in today's society.

When the term lifelong learning is literally plugged into a funding proposal or used as capstone description for a new technical-vocational programme, for example, merely to sell adult education as a product, the adult educators involved are demonstrating a proclivity for current fads which brings little credit to the field as a whole. No doubt some adult educators sincerely believe that such strategies are necessary to overcome the marginalized nature of adult education as a field of practice. Unhappily, in the process, lifelong learning as a useful guiding principle has become debased currency. It serves entrepreneurial interests that have little in common with the aspirations for adult education in the twentieth century as an important means towards social change set out by such leading figures of the field as Eduard Lindeman and Richard Tawney whose career was 'marked by an outstanding capacity to combine scholarship sighted with practical actions on a wide variety of educational and political fronts'.

Erosion of autonomous and community interests

So what important dimensions of the everyday lives of adults are being betrayed, though inadvertently, by adult educators wedded to the cult of efficiency as an orientation to pedagogical practice?

Critical dimensions of everyday life that are always threatened by the cult of efficiency can be identified, for example, in Ivan Illich's thought-provoking study on 'Vernacular Values and Education'. Here, Illich focuses primarily on how the rationalized development of spoken and written language in the West has shaped the way people experience their world in line with the bureaucratic needs of the state. Language reflects experience, and the interests of the modern state require that, in general, we experience the world within certain parameters. Illich's analysis lays out the whole arena of crucial practical and ethical values of everyday living that are being eroded by the kind of rationalization and technicist perspectives exemplified in the development of modern European languages. This development has meant the loss of important human values that are embedded in vernacular idioms. The following extracts make explicit the kind of values Illich has in mind when he evokes the idea of the vernacular:

> Vernacular comes from an Indo-Germanic root that implies 'rootedness' and 'abode'. Vernaculam as a Latin word was used for whatever was homebred, homespun, homegrown, homemade, as opposed to what was used in formal exchange... we need a simple straightforward word to designate the activities of people when they are not motivated by thoughts of exchange, a word that denotes autonomous, non-market related actions that by their very nature escape bureaucratic control, satisfying needs to which, in the very process, they give specific shape ... By speaking about vernacular language and the possibility of its recuperation, we trying to bring into awareness and discussion the existence of a vernacular mode of being, doing, and making that in a desirable future society might again expand all aspects of life.

Here, at any rate, Illich does hold out the possibility that some values and modes of being needed for autonomous lifestyles, though threatened, can be preserved and that others, already lost, might be regained. However, he again highlights the psychic damage wrought in our everyday living, and the undermining of genuine autonomous activities, by the onslaught of extreme rationalization and technicist orientations in a brilliant essay entitled 'Silence is a Commons'.

The 'commons' is a metaphor illich uses to draw attention to those traditional areas of everyday living that are so vital to our well-being. Again, it is clear from the analysis that the cult of efficiency, the inappropriate deployment of technique, is eroding this precious area of community life. Elsewhere, Jürgen Habermas, the eminent critical theorist of the Frankfurt School, has identified this phenomenon as the colonization of our life-world.

Adult educators in today's society have been remiss in not shaping their practice to help preserve the vitalistic values and practices that are continually being eroded from the pressure of those standardizing strategies embedded in the cult of efficiency. A more depressing, though perhaps realistic interpretation, is that professional adult educators are in the vanguard of those who are concerned to teach us how to embrace and cope with technicist forces that are slicing away at those values and day-to-day human activities which Ivan Illich so insightfully depicts in his essays on vernacular values and the 'commons'.

In One Dimensional Man: Studies in the Ideology of Advanced Industrial Society, Herbert Marcuse dealt with the harmful effects that technicist developments and the concomitant erosion of crucial ways of life have rendered on the psyches of modern men and women. One of Marcuse's many graphic accounts of the predicament of one-dimensional man runs as follows:

> The political needs of society become individual needs and aspirations, their satisfaction promotes business and the commonweal, and the whole appears to be the very embodiment of Reason.

Twenty year ago, Marcuse's analysis indicated that the tendency of technology to institute more effective controls was accompanied by increasing standards of living for the majority. The later prospect is no longer assured but there are now far more impressive examples to substantiate Marcuse's claim that 'the technological society is a system of domination which operates already in the concept and construction of techniques'.

Domination in the sense used by Marcuse does not require overt coercion by military and para-military force as is the case in modern totalitarian regimes. The expansion of technocracy in most Western societies makes that unnecessary. The values and opinions of a vast and, by all accounts, growing number of illiterate and semi-literate adults are readily shaped by the vested interests of technocratic society. Many of these people, usually referred to by American educators and sociologists as 'functionally illiterate', are kept in a state of immaturity. For while they can absorb information, their critical powers of insight have been left undeveloped. They really do have extreme difficulty in dealing with concepts that cannot be reduced to true and false responses. Hence, they fall prey to the simplistic television media of the President's men, carefully orchestrated commercial touting the virtues of unabashed consumerism, and the dogmatic assertion of fundamentalists who have cleverly staked out so much broadcasting time in the electronic box.

The power of television cannot be minimized. It lends itself so completely to the delivery of efficiently packaged uncomplicated messages for absorption by passive spectators. Cavalier retorts by corporate advocates of television who claim that it is predominantly a medium of entertainment are intended to defuse criticism by making it appear pompous and over-serious. This gambit should not obscure the fact that television serves to shape the experience of so many illiterate and semi-literate people, in particular as well as exerting an influence on the population at large. More and more of the former are now existing apart from the kind of community life that provides meaningful cultural alternatives. Accordingly, they rely heavily on television for their understanding of the world outside. Any protest at the way things actually are for themselves often manifests itself in ill considered and individualistic criminal acts and self-inflicted violence since their abilities to analyse, and possibly address, the structures of a technological society which shape their lives are undeveloped.

The modern practice of adult education, if not all that significantly, contributes to this state of affairs. In so far as the aim is to develop adult education into the technical design and delivery of instruction, adult education endeavours merge into the mainstream of a cult of efficiency which discourages the nurturing of genuine critical inquiry. For the most part, the relatively small proportion of illiterates served by formal adult education agencies are to be taught 'coping skills' and 'functional literacy' so that they can fit in with the unquestioned demands of a technological society.

That American adult educators, in particular, should adopt this role is not so surprising, for they too, like other professional groups, are shaprd and their behaviours guided by the norms of a technological society. Intellectuals from other countries are sometimes taken aback at the naivety of educated Americans who assume that the Great Democracy affords its citizens the possibility of a very wide range of freedoms while they are, in fact, prepared via schooling, the media, and other forms of institutionalized training to accommodate, and make themselves accountable to, quite restrictive demands of a modern capitalist society. In their quest for upward mobility a vast number of educated Americans, and this includes adult educators, accept in a taken for granted way the imposition of all manner of accountability checks and carefully designed norming techniques that encourage a preoccupation with personal development while impeding any inclination for critical appraisal of coercive structures that sustain an advanced technological society. Ironically, in more directly oppressive regimes, educated people are more likely to be aware of the official deceptions and distorted media messages which shape their everyday lives. The refusal of the Russian expatriate writer, Alexander Solzhenitsyn, a former inmate of the Gulag, to celebrate the superior freedom of the USA may seem churlish to many educated Americans. However, he is well qualified to recognize the effectiveness of those taken-for-granted techniques of control which maintain the illusion of an already achieved democracy in the United States of America. Adult educators in other Western democracies cannot reasonably derive any sense of superiority over their American colleagues if they think about the way modern adult education practice in their respective countries is defined increasingly by a technocratic ethos.

It is in this context that the modern practice of adult education must be viewed as an essentially accommodative endeavour. In their preoccupation with promoting personal and career development techniques, facilitating 'coping skills', and marketing 'functional literacy' many adult educators avoid serious engagement with those controlling social structures which block the prospects of an adult education endeavour for, and with, a genuine participatory democracy. The few adult educators who do raise questions about the coercive nature of an advanced technological society tend to be regarded as somewhat idiosyncratic. At best, their criticisms are accepted with good-humoured tolerance. After all, it is possible to accommodate a few 'radicals', 'anarchists', and highly serious academics on the periphery. They make for something a little different, an acceptable diversion to the main production-oriented concern for participation rates, courses scheduled, certificates awarded, competences achieved, continuing education units mandated, and so on. There is, with such an agenda, no time to consider seriously suggestions that a technocratically educated populace could fall nicely under the sway of any despotism.

Of course, adult educators cannot be held entirely to account for the negative developments of a technocratic society and its coercive effects as analysed by writers like Illich, Marcuse, and Habermas. However, the problems we have posed in the preceding pages begin to lay out the terrain on which an authentic vocation of adult education can be practised. In subsequent chapters we shall be identifying the kind of orientations and strategies that become contextually relevant to vocational practice. These constitute a significant role for adult educators in today's society in light of the problems we have addressed. At this juncture, though, it is important to emphasize again that we are not advocating a romanticized anti-technical stance. Rather, we are envisaging a shift in deployment, as it were, in which technological discoveries, and the methods patterned on them, are incorporated to practical needs for the enhancement of 'vernacular competence'. Technology shaped to meet practical needs rather than the expensive, often wasteful, demands of an advanced consumer society. Adult educators can make a start by refusing to be involved in the formulation and deployment of a standardized curriculum that reinforces socialization to technocratic norms.

A reliance on instrumental approaches, standardized techniques, in adult education does play a significant role in foreclosing on prospects for facilitating more genuine democratic decision-making. Yet adult education provides a legitimate context where, in face-to-face interaction, competence in the kind of rational discourse and identification of relevant information that must precede genuine democratically determined projects of action can be learned. We are referring here to learnable strategies that lead us towards what Jürgen Habermas has characterized as communicative action.

Communicative action describes an ideal, though conceivably achievable, group learning experience where participants put forward their own views on the problem at hand, listen carefully and respectfully to those of others, and seriously examine all relevantly identified information introduced to the situation. It does not take the form of a debate, or the mere weighing of pros and cons. The process is more rational and democratic—a kind of on-going, thoughtful, conversation. All participants anticipate that their individual contributions will receive serious consideration from others. At the same time, they remain open to changing or to reconstructing their own stance on the problem under consideration in the light of what others have to say and on the weight of all relevantly identified information. In this way, distortions and coercive elements that characterize so much of our normal day-to-day interaction are identified and can be eliminated of, at least, confronted for what they are. Communicative action, then, represents a worthwhile state of affairs that adult educators can seek to achieve in a wide variety of contexts. It entails a predisposition towards decision-making processes where all participants are engaged in rational discourse that emerges from a genuinely democratic situation.

If the conditions described here refer us to an ideal situation, efforts to attain it are worthwhile even though we fall short. Through such efforts we at least begin to appreciate the practical value of an inter-subjective understanding that comes from individuals being open to what others have to offer while, at the same time, being willing to present their own viewpoints for critical assessment. Such are the conditions that provide a basis for rational, genuinely democratic, decision-making. They cannot be taken for granted, and they have to be learned. The process is emancipatory in intent and does not seek foreclosure from the deployment of standardized formulations, predetermined techniques, at the outset.

Communicative action is, at one and the same time both rational and emancipatory in intent because progress towards inter-subjective agreement along the lines described is accompanied by a disclosure of coercive structures that stand in the way of arriving at projects of action formulated through a genuinely democratic process. Herein lies the challenge for adult educators. The process has to be learned through the acquisition of communicative competence. And this does not simply entail the passing on of readily definable skills. It requires practice and the willingness to analyse continuously shortfalls in practice. An important part of the on-going educative task becomes one of identifying and confronting coercive structures that obstruct, and gloss over the need for, emancipatory rational communicative action as the prime source of everyday projects of action. We shall be returning to the theme of communicative action and its importance for adult education practice.

The trappings: co-operation and consensus

In subsequent chapters we will consider adult education orientations that are in keeping with efforts to realize genuine participatory decision-making. For now, it suffices to point out that much of current adult education practice, with its heavy reliance on technicist approaches to needs assessment, programme development, and standardized curriculum design, stands in the way of the kind of emancipatory process characterized by the notion of communicative action. Unwittingly, adult educators who uncritically embrace technicist ideology are contributing to coercive effects, even where these are not immediately apparent, that obstruct emancipatory learning endeavours. The situation becomes even more depressing when we consider the way emancipatory terminology is often co-opted in the service of quite prescriptive adult learning curricula. Hence, we come across individualized learning' and 'self-paced learning' to describe bureaucratically managed, often computer steered, programmes. These present us with the anomaly of directed 'self-directed learning'.

Even techniques employed by adult educators to engender greater participation from their clients tend to be quite manipulative and militate against genuine communicative decision-making. For example, the delphi technique, is sometimes employed by adult educators in North America as a mechanism for reaching consensus. The consensus is achieved among participating adults around concerns already identified by selected experts, usually external to the immediate decision-making group. Group participants are given the opportunity to rank and rate these already identified concerns and even add to some of their own. This constitutes the first round of the process. The results are reported to the participants again in the light of data from round one. There can be a number of rounds, allowing participants a chance to rank and rate issues on the basis of information processed in the preceding round. So the technique has all the trappings of democratic procedure, evading difficult and thoughtful discussion merited by complex issues.

However, further reflection on delphi and similar consensus forming approaches reveal how easily we fall for the illusion of technique. The systematizing structures of the process define a short cut to consensus that differs altogether from communicative action which allows individual—even idiosyncratic - viewpoints of all concerned to be taken into account from the outset as part of rational discourse. It does not start off from groundwork already laid out by a specially chosen group of experts although, of course, expert knowledge is incorporated as parties to the process determine its relevance for their practical purposes. This kind of approach to rational, democratically determined, inter-subjective agreement is difficult to facilitate and will frequently fall far short of satisfactory resolution, but it suggests a far more fruitful way to go for adult educators than techniques like delphi which delude us into regarding them as truly democratic. In fact, their systematic structures and formulations, impressive though they may seem in terms of efficiency, work against the acquisition of communicative competence. They foreclose on the kind of difficult discussion required if individual and community needs are to be identified in a participatory and democratic context.

Professionalization, the cult of efficiency, and mandatory continuing education

Reference to the role of experts in the preceding paragraphs brings us to the issue of professionalization as an aspect of the cult of efficiency. Adult educators are very caught up in this issue with regard to their own practice. Advocates of professionalization in adult education point to benefits, in terms of greater legitimation for the field of practice and assurance of competence for the public at large, that are said to accrue from licensure, certification, standardized minimum criteria for preparatory training, continuing professional education and the other trappings of modern professions. These professions are often served by adult educators who design, facilitate, teach and assess continuing professional education courses.

Arguments in support of professionalization are fairly straightforward. They are advanced on the grounds that professionalization provides, on the one hand, some assurance to the public about the competence of certified experts from whom they receive services and, on the other, job and income security for members of professional groups. Efficiency, expertise, and systematic organization of practice are frequently invoked as terms to characterize professional groups, especially the most successful and monopolistic among them. Unhappily, in today's society, taken-for-granted, uncritical acceptance of the expertise and efficiency of others, supported by certification, licensing, and other forms of credentialling, has led to excessive dependence on the professionals.

A tendency of professionalization to infantilize adults in more and more arenas of everyday life exemplifies yet another way the cult of efficiency both individual autonomy and rational community values. The latter begin to be shaped by professionalized norms. For example, though it might, arguably, be appropriate for most babies to be born in hospital, how many women would even begin to consider the benefits of giving birth to their children at home, even with help from a competent mid-wife, in view of the 'high tech' expertise of over busy, though wonderfully organized medical doctors of Western society? To ensure that not too much serious thought of rational alternatives to professionalized birthing occurs, the medical profession in North America has the support, at present, of the legal profession, which can outlaw such alternatives in modern society. At best, the cult of efficiency that sustains the medical profession makes the few women who opt to avoid professionalized birthing appear idiosyncratic.

Even though we could identify numerous instances of how professionalization has fostered irrational dependence, it is scarcely feasible to think in terms of a sustained programme that would de-professionalize modern society to the extent envisaged by Ivan Illich in De-schofeling Society. However, adult education has fallen short in not identifying and facilitating strategies whereby we can resist the further inappropriate encroachment of professionalization into our everyday lives and roll back its most repressive effects. This would entail creating an awareness of those activities and services which adults as individuals, or in groups, could undertake without placing themselves entirely in the hands of experts. Recourse to professionals would be relevantly determined as an intelligent option rather than as an automatic, taken-for-granted, course of action. At the same time as identifying practical strategies to retrieve human services from the monopolistic domain of professionalism, the adult education movement as a whole, not just a few academic critics, should have been at the forefront in raising questions about the legitimacy and rationality of moves in the direction of further professionalization in modern society and within the field of adult education itself.

The home-schooling and alternative community-based schooling movement is an example of where adults, for reasons which vary from one family to another, have selected for their children an alternative to the professionalized teaching of the state schools. It is not necessary to hold out for the entire de-schooling of society in order to resist monopolistic claims on expertise by professionalized educationalists. Parents of home-schoolers, and those educated in alternative community-based schools, are chiefly concerned about the well-being of their children but, at the same time, they are resisting the claims of this officially supported aspect of the cult of efficiency to determine the shape of their children's education. For them schooling becomes a matter of choice, not an official mandate.

Rather than supporting people towards authentic alternatives to a lifestyle that has become increasingly dependent on professionalized services at every turn, modern practitioners of adult education, especially in the United States and Canada, tend to concern themselves with enhancing the knowledge base of professionals. The notion is that this focus guarantees further efficient service to the public. But it is not just a matter of ensuring designated experts become more competent. An unchecked trend towards strengthening professionalized interests in society is accompanied by an erosion of autonomy in our everyday lives. Monopolistic tendencies of professionalized groups signify a de-skilling of the majority who are prevented from providing services in the professionalized domains for themselves and for others. This leads to greater dependence on the state apparatus and well organized vested interests.

We could argue, with considerable force, that it is neither possible nor desirable to dispense with the convenience of specialized services delivered by designated experts. However, it is feasible to envisage reversing some of the deleterious effects on today's society of an excessive tendency towards professionalism, reducing the widespread dependence it engenders. Further, it is reasonable to suggest that adult educators, on the whole, have been remiss in not confronting the serious consequences for the everyday lives of adults that stem from encroaching professionalization. Those adult educators who confine their commitment to the training of careerist professionals actually add fuel to a crisis that results from a cult of efficiency. When adult educators allow themselves a preoccupation with the professionalization of their own endeavours, they become very much part of the problem and abandon any real prospect of achieving an emancipatory, critical practice of adult education.

Unfortunately, the issue of professionalization is woven into the fabric of adult education practice in today's society. And it spoils the cloth. For professionalization with its array of legitimizing artifacts is, if anything, more problematic for the practice of adult education in today's society than its most determined critics have suggested.

The entire edifice of professionalization is sustained by the mechanisms of certification, licensing, and accreditation. Further, any really meaningful distinctions between these three legitimizing practices have become blurred. The ostensible purpose of certification, licensing, and accreditation is to give some assurance to society at large as to the quality of services provided by professionals while providing them with job security. However, to an extent which varies from one profession to another, these legitimizing mechanisms also confer monopolistic privileges on professionals. The amount of power, autonomy, and exclusivity accumulated by a particular professional group is discernible from how successful it has been in deploying the legitimizing mechanisms of certification, licensing, and accreditation to signify a clear-cut body of knowledge. This becomes, for the most powerful professions, an exclusive domain of well defined techniques in which only officially designed experts can lawfully practise. Clearly, medical doctors, for example, have been more successful in this regard than public school teachers. Up to now, associations of medical doctors have managed to keep the legitimizing mechanisms for determining who shall or shall not be permitted to practise within their own hands, and they have been relatively successful in thwarting attempts by others to carve out professions within the wide domain of medical care. The case of the medical profession, in particular, demonstrates how professional preparation is tied in to mechanisms of systematic legitimation which confer power and monopolistic privileges on doctors that are not in themselves demonstrably warranted as the only practical way to satisfy the health and medical needs of the populace.

In addition to bestowing power and monopolistic privileges on professionals, certification, licensing and credentialling are widely viewed as indicators of technical competence. Therefore, in order to keep step with the continuing surge of technical innovations, it has become necessary to support their function as legitimizing mechanisms through mandatory continuing professional education. If they want to retain their licences more and more professionals are being compelled to take continuing education, though thoughtful writers both for and against mandatory continuing education agree that it cannot be shown to guarantee competent performance. Even if it were possible to demonstrate a convincing causal connection between mandatory continuing education and concomitant performance, there are some who would continue to question, from an ethical standpoint, the whole business of forcing adults back to school. For them mandatory continuing education represents yet another stage in the surrender of individual autonomy, an invasion of personal discretionary time, to the stipulations of a technical rationality. It is true that many professionals are in favour of mandatory continuing education on the grounds that it obliges them to keep up to date. The questions that might arise about what this acquiescence says of a mature commitment to their work and a willingness to undertake relevant continuing education on their own initiative tend to be overlooked. Further, it is important to consider, in a wider ethical context, the significance of this cavalier acquiescence on the part of relatively privileged professionals for less powerful members of our society. If doctors, dentists, and lawyers are willing to accept mandatory continuing education, what right have welfare recipients to even question having to go back to school in order to maintain eligibility for their monthly cheques? The willing surrender of autonomy in many significant area of everyday life, and by one influential societal group does have ripple effects on other social contexts.

Mandatory continuing education is not just confined to professional groups: an entire corpus of literature on the topic, both for and against, has served to make it an issue among adult educators in the United States and Canada, where mandatory continuing education has been in vogue for longer and is more widespread than in other countries. Unfortunately, the earnestness required to keep dialogue open in the face of burgeoning mandatory continuing education initiatives begins to flag. Not surprisingly, critics tend to become disheartened, preferring to retire from the fray rather than continuing to sustain a critical analysis which is too readily dismissed, in the context of an overarching cult of efficiency, as tiresome and utopian. Yet it is important that the issue of mandatory continuing education remains problematic. Without sustained questioning on ethical and practical grounds, the discourse of a technical rationality which justifies implementation of mandatory stipulations because they might lead to greater efficiency and overall competence soon becomes taken for granted. Despite the number of thoughtful essays which question mandatory continuing education, there is a powerful inclination to feel that the questioners have had their day and that the real task ahead is to deploy mandatory continuing education programmes as effectively as possible. This inclination to foreclose on critical analysis and to discourage further resistance is unfortunate. It begins to appear that the rationality of mandatory education measures has prevailed over a more democratic disposition to enshrine voluntary participation in adult education. Thus, the way is open for an expansion of scarcely examined policies that support the compulsory education of adults.

The difficulty is that the discourse of technical rationality which justifies the introduction of coercive measures for efficiency's sake has a momentum all of its own. It can flourish without the help of adult educators, who can best provide the kind of ethical and practical questioning which keeps open the prospect of genuine emancipatory practice in all dimensions of everyday life. This should include educational initiatives that enable people to make more practical decision in areas of everyday life currently dominated by the professions. The professions themselves are continuously and systematically involved in professionalizing measures which include the adoption of mandatory continuing education. This activity will continue space without mediation and encouragement from adult educators.

The cachet that attaches to the professions might appeal to some practitioners and university professors working in a marginalized field such as adult education. If helping with the actual professionalization process is their goal, a most relevant course of action for them would seem to lie within the professionalized sphere as a credentialized member of a profession. A more appropriate role for adult educators with regard to professionalization can be enacted in providing critical discourse and approaches to practice which differ from the largely non-reflective technical discourse and depersonalized orientation to practice of professionals. The means to demystifying the technical discourse and practice of professionalized groups are divided from critical analysis predisposed to favour ethical and practical terminology over the argot of technique. By and large adult educators, practitioners and academics alike, have not been inclined to sustain a continuing rational critique of professionalized practice either in written form or in their everyday discourse. There are, on the contrary, more signs of an eagerness among adult educators to take on the trappings of professionalized associations.

Very little, then, in the way of educative strategies on how we can retrieve some of those responsibilities for our lives abrogated to professionals has emerged from the ranks of adult educators. And it is not as though there are no clearly identifiable social groups who would be prepared to consider seriously such strategies. More and more people are finding that there are practical alternatives to public schooling for their children. Alternative approaches to the maintenance of individual and community health are being explored outside of the professionalized sphere, and it is becoming more apparent that legal knowledge is not all in the hands of credentialized lawyers even though they have shaped the entire discourse and practice of law. At the very least, there is a considerable role for adult educators to play in informing adults of how to ask relevant questions of the professionals whose services they seek so that they can retain as much autonomy as possible within the professional/client encounter. Wealthy, powerful people are better at it than the poor and under-educated.

However, in today's society, self-help groups and co-operative initiatives that gain momentum become a focus of attention for professionals who operate in the same sphere of activity; for example, doctors with regard to medical self-help groups. Although often welcome, this can lead to intervention for the best of rational, professionalized interests. Co-operation between high status professionals and volunteer groups is an appealing notion. However, any formalized relationships between professional associations and volunteer groups need to be viewed as problematic. They can too readily form the context for subverting any prospects for retrieving some of the lost autonomy in our everyday lives which Illich characterized as the 'commons'.

The metaphor of the 'commons' sets out the context where the crisis for adult education is most apparent. To the extent that adult educators lend themselves to efforts which lead to the erosion of the 'commons', adult education becomes, at best, appraisal, redundant as a distinctive area of practice. Professionalizing trends based on a technicist rationality will bring in technological innovations and technocratic practice without any mediation from adult educators. There is, however, a very vital role for adult educators to play in retrieving bits of the 'commons', and in working to resist further erosion through a critical pedagogy. This entails maintaining a high level of ethically based critical discourse and practice on behalf of less empowered groups in society, and on the avoidance of uncritical acceptance of technocratic innovation to the adult education endeavour. An anti-technicist stance is not ani-technological, nor is it against the acquisition of technical competence. It places priority on an ethos which requires that any deployment of technological innovations, technical programmes, and expertise be steered by practical and relevant interests, both emancipatory and instrumental, of the least empowered majority in today's society.

2 Adult Learners: Motives for Learning and Practice

When adults teach and learn in one another's company, they find themselves engaging in a challenging, passionate, and creative activity. The acts of teaching and learning-and the creation and alteration of our beliefs, values, actions, relationships, and social forms that result from this-are ways in which we realize our humanity. The extent to which adults are engaged in a free exchange of ideas, beliefs, and practices is one gauge of whether a society is open, democratic, and healthy. If adults of widely differing class and ethnic groups are actively exploring ideas, beliefs, and practices, then we are likely to have a society in which creativity, diversity, and the continuous re-creation of social structures are the accepted norms. By contrast, societies in which inquiry, reflection, and exploration are the prerogative of a privileged minority are likely to be static, ossified, and hierarchical.

It would be easy for professional educators to translate the above argument into a declaration that a society can be considered healthy to the extent that it provides publicly funded learning opportunities for adults. This may be one indicator of a just society, but it is not the only one and it neglects the enormous amount of significant adult learning, individual and collective, that takes place outside formal educational settings. The teaching-learning transactions undertaken by adults are complex and multifaceted, and they steadfastly refuse simple categorization. They occur in every setting imaginable, are conducted at different levels of significance to the learner, are oriented toward a variety of cognitive, affective, psychomotor, and political ends, and involve a range of formats and methods.

In all these instances, several commonalities are observable. At a very basic level, of course, the participants involved are adults: that is, they have attained the legal and chronological status of adulthood. Second, they are engaged in a purposeful exploration of a field of knowledge or set of skills or in a collective reflection upon common experiences. Third, these explorations of knowledge, skills, and experiences take place in a group setting. Fourth, the participants in these explorations bring to the encounter a collection of experiences, skills, and knowledge that are going to influence how new ideas are received, how new skills are acquired, and how the experiences of others are interpreted. As Gange has observed, every adult's stock of prior learning and experience coheres into a unique, idiosyncratic mediatory mechanism through which new experiences and knowledge are filtered. Hence, as educators we can never predict with total certainty how one adult will respond to being presented with new ideas, interpretations, skill sets, experiences, or materials. Fifth, such prior learning and experience also comprise valuable curricular resources. In the examples of the teaching-learning transactions mentioned earlier, the topics discussed, themes explored, experiences interpreted, skills acquired, and knowledge investigated will be influenced by, and will draw upon, this prior learning and experience. The tenants, managers, school principals, shop stewards, single parents, and nonreaders will identify common problems, voice common concerns, specify skills in which they feel that they are deficient, and provide experiences upon which others in the group can reflect.

Finally, the transactions in these groups will be characterized by a respect for individual members that will be manifest in the procedures used. These groups will probably use discussion methods that will allow individual members' contributions to be jointly interpreted and explored; and, if the group leader is acting as a good facilitator, no one member will be cajoled, insulted, or intimidated by the pressure of majority opinion. Leadership of some of these groups will be rotational, and individual members will, at different times and for different purposes, assume temporary leadership of the group. Even where an appointed leader is present, it is likely that he or she will feel no sense of professional dereliction in surrendering "authority" to allow group members to voice concerns, change the curricular focus, and alter previously agreed-upon rules of group conduct. Integral to this climate of respect for individual members is an expectation that the teaching-learning process will be distinguished by a continual negotiation of objectives, methods, and evaluative criteria.

Principles of effective practice

Before proceeding to further discussion of facilitating learning, we should clarify the central principles of effective practice. These principles apply chiefly to teaching-learning transactions or to curriculum development and instructional design activities that support teaching-learning encounters and not to marketing, budgetary, or administrative tasks.

Let us consider, then, the following six principles of effective practice in facilitating learning:

- Participation in learning is voluntary; adults engage in learning as a result of their own volition. It may be that the circumstances prompting this learning are external to the learner but the decision to learn is the learner's. Hence, excluded are those settings in which adults are coerced, bullied, or intimidated into learning.
- Effective practice is characterized by a respect among participants for each others self-worth. Foreign to facilitation are behaviors, practices or statements that belittle others or that involve emotional or physical abuse. This does not mean that criticism should be absent from educational encounters. It does mean though

that an attention to increasing adults' sense of self-worth underlies all facilitation efforts.

- Facilitation is collaborative. Facilitators and learners are engaged in a cooperative enterprise in which, at different times and for different purposes, leadership and facilitation roles will be assumed by different group members. This collaboration is seen in the diagnosis of needs in the setting of objectives, in curriculum development, in methodological aspects, and in generating evaluative criteria and indexes. This collaboration is also constant, so that the group process involves a continual renegotiation of activities and priorities in which competing claims are explored, discussed, and negotiated.

- Praxis is placed at the heart of effective facilitation. Learners and facilitators are involved in a continual process of activity, reflection upon activity, collaborative analysis of activity, new activity, further reflection and collaborative analysis, and so on. "Activity" can,of course, include cognitive activity; learning does not always require participants to "do" something in the sense of performing clearly observable acts. Exploring a wholly new way of interpreting one's work, personal relationship, or political allegiances would be an example of activity in the sense.

- Facilitation aims to foster in adults a spirit of critical reflection. Through educational encounters, learners come to appreciate that values, beliefs, behaviors, and ideologies are culturally transmitted and that they are provisional and relative. This awareness that the supposed givens of work conduct, relationship, and political allegiances are, in fact, culturally constructed means that adults will come to question many aspects of their professional, personal, and political lives.

- The aim of facilitation is the nurturing of self-directed, empowered adults. Such adults will see themselves as proactive, initiating individuals engaged in a continuous re-creation of their personal relationship, work worlds, and social circumstances rather than as reactive individuals, buffeted by uncontrollable forces of circumstance.

These six principles of facilitation have numerous implications for practice that will be discussed throughout this book. They are observable in many different settings, some of which are formally called "adults" or "continuing" education, some of which are designated as "training," and others that are recognized by other descriptions. In general terms, though, a number of direct practice implications are immediately derivable from each principle.

Voluntary Participation. The fact that adults engage in an educational activity because of some innate desire for developing new skills, acquiring new knowledge, improving already assimilated competencies, or sharpening powers of self-insight has enormous implications for what facilitators can do. First and foremost, the educator has no need to spend a great deal of time and energy dealing with outright defiance, veiled opposition, or studied indifference among learners. Those who teach adults in the evening and children or adolescents during the day constantly refer to the difference in satisfaction, and fulfillment derived from working with the two groups. Because adults' motivations to learn are high, the facilitator is prompted to expend a similarly high level of effort and ingenuity in designing educational experiences and in teaching. Adults' willingness to learn also means that they are less likely to resist participatory learning techniques such as discussion, role playing, games, small-groups work, and collaborative analysis of personal experiences.

The voluntary nature of participation by adult learners also means that such participation can easily be withdrawn if learners feel that the activity dose not meet their needs, does not make any particular sense, or is conducted at a level that is incomprehensible to them. The same holds true, of course, if learners feel that they are being treated in a humiliating or insulting manner. Facilitators thus have to pay close attention to curriculum development and educational process. Curricular themes for examination and topics to be discussed have to be grounded in adults' experiences, or at the very least there must be explicit connections made between unfamiliar concepts or bodies of knowledge and the current preoccupations for past experiences of learners.

This can be done by selecting appropriate resource materials and by framing the investigation of new ideas, skills, or information in terms that are accessible to the learner, given his or her past experiences.

The importance of ensuring that new knowledge, concepts, skills, or frameworks of interpretation are presented to adult learners in a manner that is comprehensible in terms of their own experiences is a major reason for using participatory learning methods. A mass instructional technique such as a lecture may, as Bligh notes, be useful in presenting information in short, twenty-minute periods. As a host of research studies cited by Bligh indicate, however, the lecture is of little use if the educator or trainer is seeking to promote critical thinking or to encourage adults to be more flexible in their attitudes. A one hour transmission of information in which there is no opportunity for questions, no small-groups discussion of case-study applications of ideas, no "buzz group" activity, and no attempt to make connections between the audience members' experiences and the lecture's content is, therefore, poor facilitation. Educators who ignore the use of participatory techniques will find that their learners are physically absent in increasing numbers or are mentally absent in the sense of not being actively engaged with the ideas, skill, and knowledge being presented.

Mutual respect. A fundamental feature of effective facilitation is to make participants feel that they are valued as separate, unique individuals deserving of respect. To behave in a manner disrespectful to others, to denigrate their contributions, or to embarrass them publicly through extended attention to their apparent failings are behaviors that are, in educational terms, disastrous. Educators who behave in this manner will be faced with a number of consequences. They will find participants leaving, they will be unable to generate the goodwill required to conduct effective participatory learning exercises, and they will find learners so intimidated by the prospect of public pillorying or private censure that they will be unable to learn. Many of the same consequences will result if educators allow learners to behave toward one another in hostile or combative ways.

Good facilitation, then, is characterized by a respect for participants' uniqueness, self-worth, and separateness. This does not mean, however, that educational encounters are characterized by some kind of universal bonhomie or false camaraderie under which fundamental differences are buried. Central to the effective facilitation of learning is the development of powers of critical reflection, and this means that adults will frequently be challenged by educators and fellow learners to consider alternative ways of thinking, behaving, working, and living. But this challenging of others' ideas and attitudes and this prompting of analysis of one's own behaviors and beliefs must occur in a setting where dissension or criticism of another does not imply some kind of personal denigration. As Brew has observed with regard to discussion groups, it is easy for educational encounters to degenerate into "numbers of people slamming shut their minds in one another's faces". Unless participants evolve what Bridges calls a "moral culture" governing educational interactions, then learners will react to being challenged or to being confronted with alternative and unfamiliar ways of thinking about their work, relationships, or beliefs with resistance and a dismissive mistrust.

One of the most daunting and difficult tasks of the facilitator, then, is to set a climate for learning and to assist in the development of a group culture in which adults can feel free to challenge one another and can feel comfortable with being challenged. Without such a climate or culture, teaching-learning encounters run the risk of becoming nothing more than exchanges of entrenched opinion and prejudice, with no element of challenge and no readiness to probe the assumptions underlying beliefs, behaviors, or values. It is useless to run a staff development workshop in which participants compliment each other, repeat the public norms of the organization, and confirm prejudices but never address fundamental differences in philosophy or practice. What is valuable, however, is the honest expression of differences, in an atmosphere where challenge and dissension are accepted as part of the educational process.

Collaborative spirit. The existence of some kind of participatory and collaborative element is perhaps the most frequently cited difference between school education and the education of adults. In the former, standards, syllabi, materials, and evaluative criteria are generally externally defined according to local or national governmental regulations and requirements. In the latter, principally because formal accreditation or certification is not the aim of most adult education programmes, there is often collaboration in assessing needs and generating objectives, methods of learning and evaluative procedures. There is also an alternation of educational roles so that at different times various members of the adult learning group will assume responsibility for posing questions, identifying materials, suggesting priorities, and organizing aspects of the group process.

Such collaborative activities are, of course, grounded in the features of voluntary learning and respect for participants. Acknowledging the accumulated experiences of adults as valuable educational resources is frequently touted as a defining principle of adult education, but this can be achieved only through some collaborative medium. The distinct tradition in the facilitation of adult learning is that of adults meeting as equals in small groups to explore issues and concerns and then to take action as a result of these explorations. We can see this in the workers' education movement, the junto, community development initiatives such as the Antigonish movement, community action projects in Liverpool and Northern Ireland the living room learning groups in British Columbia experiments using mass media such as the Canadian Farm Forum BBC wireless discussion groups and the Great Books program as well as in the establishment of residential centers for community development such as the Highlander Folk School and the Ulster People's College .

Action and reflection. In the education and training of adults, the term praxis is closely associated with the ideas and literacy activities of Brazilian educator, Paulo Freire. In several works he discusses a number of specific techniques that were used to help South American illiterates acquire literacy skills. In developing these skills, learners would gradually become aware of forces and structures that were keeping them in a position of dependence. Central to this concept, however, is a process long ago recognized as fundamentally educational by such philosophers of education as Dewey and Neill. This process centers on the need for educational activity to engage the learner in a continuous and alternating process of investigation and exploration, followed by action grounded in this exploration, followed by reflection on this action, followed by further investigation and exploration, followed by further action, and so on. This notion of praxis as alternating and continuous engagements by teachers and learners in exploration, action, and reflection is central to adult learning. It means that exploration of new ideas, skills, or bodies of knowledge do not take place in a vacuum but are set within the context of learners' past, current, and future experiences.

In settings where skills are being learned, whether literacy skills, craft skills, or political advocacy techniques, this praxis is easily observable. Learners become acquainted with skills, apply these in real life settings, reflect with other learners on their experiences in these settings, redefine how these skills might be altered by context, reapply these in other real settings, and so on. This is the familiar mechanism of internships and field experience as used in numerous training settings.

In activities concerned primarily with changes in consciousness, attitudinal shifts, explorations of new interpretations of the world, or paradigm shifts of some kind, the same principle of praxis obtains. In these instances, the process is less easily observable as it occurs chiefly through the acquisition of new mental sets. Even here, however, it is hard to imagine anything other than the purest form of philosophical meditation or introspection occurring without the learner's renegotiating certain aspects of his or her relationship, social world, or work life. Adults do not acquire and internalize ideas, skills, knowledge, and insights in a context-free vacuum. They interpret these through the mediatory mechanisms they have developed, assign meaning to them, codify them according to categories they have evolved, and test them out in real life settings. In curriculum design, selection of materials, and use of educational methods, therefore, facilitators should anticipate, and build upon, this tendency of adult learners to interpret, understand, codify, and assign meaning to new ideas, insights, skills, and knowledge in the context of their own experiences.

Critical reflection. That effective practice aims to foster an attitude of healthy skepticism is a prescriptively based notion, and, as such, it is disputed by some practitioners. They argue that facilitation means assisting adults to acquire skills, knowledge, ideas, and insights that have been defined by the learners themselves. This latter idea is said to exemplify a democratic, student-entered approach to learning, since it assigns to learners the responsibility for assessing needs, identifying educational aims and objectives, and generating evaluative criteria.

Facilitating learning is, however, a collaborative enterprise, and this has implications for more formal settings where the role of "educator" can be clearly identified. In these setting the educator's values and priorities will influence the educational encounter just as do those of the learners. It is my contention that learning is being effectively facilitated when the educator is prompting in learners a sense of the culturally constructed nature of knowledge, beliefs, values, and behaviours. But to develop this awareness, the facilitator must present alternative interpretations of learners' work lives, personal relationships, and views of the social and political world. this does not mean that the facilitator must try to convert or brainwash learners into accepting some new ideology. It does mean, though, that education must be distinguished from training. In training, a set of clearly identified skills are transmitted, and adults are required to assimilate these in the manner prescribed by the trainer, employing agency, or certification body. In education, by contrast, learners are encouraged to examine the assumptions underlying the acquisition of skills, to consider alternative purposes, and to place skill acquisition in some broader context.

This is very far from assuming, however, that learning cannot be facilitated effectively in training contexts. In the field of adult basic education, there are many instances in which educators have placed the acquisition of pre-defined skills in a context that encouraged learners to develop a critically questioning frame of mind. Such an attitude lies at the heart of Freirean methods and is exemplified in practical activities such as work with the elderly community education, work with college students, the promotion of industrial democracy and work with immigrant women in industrial societies. Manuals of basic education and studies of illiterates stress the development of a positive self-concept, the feeling of self-confidence, and the affirmation of self-esteem that result from coming to view the world differently through learning a language.

The point is that education is centrally concerned with the development of a critically aware frame of mind, not with the uncritical assimilation of previously defined skills or bodies of knowledge. Even within staff development or training activities that seem to be defined by organizational priorities, rather than by the learning benefits acquiring to individuals, there is a realization that encouraging shop floor workers, line managers, supervisors, and executives to challenge existing norms, practices, and structures is essential. Analyses of human resource development, staff development manuals investigations into conditions for corporate success ,and studies of effective learning within organizations all stress the necessity for workers to be aware of underlying assumptions, norms, and uncritically accepted practices and to be encouraged to imagine alternative structures and practices. The eight lessons derived from an analysis of America's most successful companies include a willingness to experiment, and engagement in praxis, participatory involvement of all employees, and managers' acknowledgement of ambiguity. Similarly, the concepts of double-loop learning and deuterolearning developed by Argyris and Schon focus on the ability of workers to become aware of underlying norms, policies, and objectives, to view these as relative and determined by context, and hence to be proactive in advocating change and innovation.

Self-direction. The last principle of effective facilitation—that facilitators should assist adults to become self-directed learners-has now attained something of the status of an academic orthodoxy. As kidd has written, "It has often been said that the purpose of adult education, or of any kind of education, is to make of the subject a continuing 'inner-directed,' self-operating learner". This idea has been proposed by educators from Lindeman and Bryson to Rogers and Knowles. It is one of adult education's most enduring articles of faith, and, like many revered tenets, its meaning has been distorted or skewed by those who choose to define it as they wish. As recent critical re-examinations have made clear, self-direction as a concept runs the risk of being denuded of context and of coming to be viewed solely as a technique in much the same way as programmed learning is now conceived.

The body of research, practice, and theoretical speculation on self-directed learning will be reviewed later in this book, so an extended analysis at this point is inappropriate. It is important to say, however, that making adults self-directed learners does not simply mean assisting them to develop such skills as how to retrieve information or locate resources. Self-direction in learning is not a set of techniques that can be applied within a context of objectives and evaluative criteria that are determined by others. At the heart of self-directedness is the adult's assumption of control over setting educational goals and generating personally meaningful evaluative criteria. One cannot be a fully self-directed learner if one is applying techniques of independent study within a context of goals and evaluative criteria determined by an external authority. Self-directed learning in adulthood, therefore, is not merely learning how to apply techniques of resource location or instructional design. It is, rather, a matter of learning how to change our perspectives, shift our paradigms, and replace one way of interpreting the world by another.

As adults, we are generally enclosed within our own self-histories. We assimilate and gradually integrate behaviors, ideas, and values derived from others until they become so internalized that we define "ourselves" in terms of them. Unless an external source places before us alternative ways of thinking, behaving, and living, we are comfortable with our familiar value systems, beliefs, and behaviors. Teachers who rely on the same exercises and notes for thirty years, managers who continue to employ the same techniques of production organization, or programmers who run the same courses year after year are not going to decide to change these practices simply of their own volition. One task of the facilitator, therefore, is to present learners with alternatives to their current ways of thinking, behaving, and living. Adults who engage in this kind of double-loop learning in which they reflect critically on their assumptions and try to imagine alternatives are fully autonomous, self-directed learners. Such adults are likely to be involved in a continual reinterpretation, renegotiation, and re-creation of their personal relationships, work lives, and social structures.

Transactional dialogues

It will be clear from the foregoing discussion, and from descriptions of practice in later chapters, that there are two common approaches to thinking about the facilitation of learning. One of these we might recognize as an operational approach. In this approach, we regard as effective practice any activity in which adults are being taught how to acquire certain skills and knowledge, irrespective of content and context. If adults are learning, and others are arranging the conditions of instruction, then we are witnessing effective facilitation.

A contrasting approach to the facilitation of learning views effective practice not just as helping adults acquire skills and knowledge in a context—and content-free manner but as containing some intrinsic features regarding the process and content of teaching and learning. Hence, educational encounters in which learners are abused or intimidated or racial prejudices are encouraged would not be regarded as facilitation in its fullest sense. Neither would we regard as good practice those instances in which adult learners are reproduced in the image of the facilitator, that is, when they mirror his or her ideas and beliefs exactly and demonstrate no capacity for critical reflection. Finally, this approach would exclude activities in which the learner is given no say in the method, aims, or content of the teaching-learning transaction and in which any deviation from a preset facilitator norm is met with exclusion from the educational activity.

This alternative approach is an intrinsic approach: It recognizes that education is value based and that facilitators should therefore be explicit concerning the values on which their ideas of good practice are based. The basis for this second approach is that education is credentially a transactional encounter in which learners and teachers are engaged in a continual process of negotiation of priorities, methods, and evaluative criteria. Viewing teaching-learning encounters as transactional means that the sole responsibility for determining curricula or for selecting appropriate methods does not rest either with the educator or with the participants. If the first obtains, then we have an authoritarian style and a one-way transmission of knowledge and skills that exemplifies all the worst aspects of the banking system of education or what Lindeman called the additive process, whereby the teacher receives from students precisely what has already been imparted from the teacher's academic repository, and the educator retains total control over the goals, content, and evaluative criteria of the educational activity. If the second approach prevails and curricula, methods, and evaluative criteria become determined solely by what learners say they want, then we run the risk that a service rationale or a "cafeteria" approach will govern what passes for education. If the educator simply meets those needs articulated by groups and individuals, he or she may function as little more than an administrator, publicist, and budget specialist. Skills of administration, marketing, and financial management are certainly important in order to create the conditions under which teaching and learning can occur. We should be careful, however, of confusing the exercise of those skills with the sum total of what it means to be an effective facilitator.

Accepting the felt needs rationale and giving learners what they say they want mean that the facilitator has abdicated responsibility for contributing to the debate about normative standards, values, and criteria in training and education. To say one is meeting felt learner needs sounds humanistic, learner centered, and admirably democratic, yet to do so without allowing one's own ideas, experience, insights, and knowledge as an educator to contribute to the educational process makes the facilitator a service manager, not a fully participating contributor. It also condemns learners to staying within their own paradigms of thinking, feeling, and behaving. Since it is very difficult to generate alternative ways of thinking about, and behaving in, the world entirely as a result of one's own efforts, an important task of the facilitator is to present to learners diverse ways of thinking and acting.

One of the greatest myths that has sprung from an acceptance of the felt needs rationale is the belief that learning is always joyful, a bountiful release of latent potential in which the learner is stimulated, exhilirated, and fulfilled. This often happens. But it also often the case that the most significant learning we undergo as adults results from some external event or stimulus that causes us to engage in an anxiety-producing and uncomfortable reassessment of aspects of our personal, occupational, and recreational lives. This external stimulus may be a calamitous event, such as being fired, experiencing the death of a parent, sibling, or spouse, going to war, our coping with a divorce. The learning in which we are forced to engage as a result of these events may be unsought and may have many painful aspects. Nonetheless, we may regard such learning as highly significant, precisely because it caused us to question our ways of thinking and behaving in our personal relationships, occupational lives, or social activities. Such questioning is initially uncomfortable and may be resisted, but it will often be the cause of our deciding to change some aspect of our lives. As anybody who has renegotiated an intimate relationship, who has confronted a parent, or who has attempted to change the patterns of relationships and activities in the workplace knows, to question the validity of the assumptions under which he or she has been living and to try to change the habitual activities and responses of oneself and others are not always joyous, releasing, and exhilarating experiences. We may conclude after this act of learning that the pain and anxiety were worthwhile, since they resulted in our living more fulfilling and stimulating lives. But as we are forced to undergo this reexamination of values, beliefs, behaviors, and assumptions about ourselves and those around us, we may find the activity to be an unsettling, painful struggle in which glimpses of insight alternate with confusion, uncertainty, and ambiguity.

The contribution of the facilitator to the

teaching-learning transaction is somewhat of the order of the calamitous events mentioned earlier. It is not enough for educators and trainers to say to learners, "Do what you want, learn what you want, in whatever manner you wish, because you are the sole determinants of your educational destinies." This resembles a conversation in which one partner agrees with whatever the other says. Such conversations may be initially agreeable, but eventually one begins to suspect that the listener who responds to one's every comment and suggestion with enthusiastic agreement is not really listening at all. A conversation, after all, is also a transactional dialogue in which the comments and contributions of the participants build organically on each other's views and in which alternative viewpoints, differing interpretations, and criticism are elements essential to the encounter.

We may think of facilitation in much the same way, as a transactional dialogue between participants who bring to the encounter experiences, attitudinal sets, and alternative ways of looking at their personal, professional, political, and recreational worlds, along with a multitude of differing purposes, orientations, and expectations. The particular function of the facilitator is to challenge learners with alternative ways of interpreting their experience and to present to them ideas and behaviors that cause them to examine critically their values, ways of acting, and the assumptions by which they live.

We should note here that there is an enormous difference between facilitation and attempts at political or religious conversion in that in the latter activities the political or religious ideologies have predetermined the learning outcomes of the activity. They possess an ideology that they feel comprises the one true way of living in and thinking about the world, and views that do not coincide with these ideologies are deemed to be examples of bad faith, false consciousness, or wrong thinking. In effective facilitation, by contrast, the educator may hold beliefs about how people should think and act that he or she passionately espouses, but such beliefs are presented to learners for the same critical scrutiny and analysis that the participants apply to ideas of which the educator is personally critical. The end of the encounter, in other words, has not been preordained as the acceptance by participants of the facilitator's values and beliefs. Educators would be foolish to deny that they possess their own beliefs or to pretend that they are blank pages on which philosophies and values are yet to be written.

3 Adult Development

Adult educators, who in many respects are critical consumers of ideas about teaching and learning, seem to have a weakness when it comes to critically evaluating theory and research in adult development. This weakness is perhaps due to the belief that the identity of adult education is promissed on the identity of the adult. Hence the literature on adult development is attractive because it offers the promise of a distinct and coherent theory of adult learning.

Published accounts of the adult learning process nearly always make reference to life-span developmental stages, the life cycle of the 'phases' of adult life. In a similar way many policy documents in adult and continuing education stress the importance of addressing the needs associated with adult development and growth. Allman sets out the case for this interest in adult development. She observes that studies of adult life reveal it to be a period of change and development, much like that of childhood and adolescence. She argues that the results of such studies serve notice on the prevailing assumptions about adulthood—that it is a long period of stability where previously learned capacities, skills, attitudes and values are applied to one's activities at work, in the family, in leisure and in civic life. These assumptions need to be challenged because they 'clearly affect decision makers in the field of politics, education and social policy'. In education they are linked to the conventional view that the period of initial education equips young adults for the remainder of their working lives - a view which continues to inform political debate on educational priorities.

Arguments like these are convincing and we do need to revise our outmoded views about adult life. But, as we shall argue we need to proceed with caution, otherwise there is a risk of replacing one set of false beliefs with another equally false set of beliefs about adult development.

This chapter reviews some of the connections which have been made between adult development and adult education. The second part focuses on evaluating the adequacy of existing theory and research in this area.

A question commonly posed by those with an interest in adult learning is 'What are the implications of adult development for adult and continuing education practitioners?' Knox outlines three possible implications:

1 To predict and explain success in education: 'Practitioners are typically interested in developmental generalizations regarding performance or personality in order to predict

and explain successful participation in educative activity'.

2 To help people adapt to changing adult roles: 'Adult life cycle trends in performance in family, occupational and community roles suggest ways in which continuing education participation might facilitate adaptation and growth related to each role area'.

3 To improve the effectiveness of marketing and instructional activities: 'From time to time, the stability of adulthood is punctuated by role change events such as the birth of the first child, a move to another community or retirement... Such change events typically produce heightened readiness to learn which, if recognized, can contribute to the effectiveness of marketing and instructional activities'.

The whole tenor of the above implications indicates a view about adult development and an attitude to adult education. That is, that the various 'roles' of adult life are inevitable and people must learn to cope with them as they arise; and that adult education agencies, if they wish to be successful, should gear their marketing and instructional activities to cater for the different needs of adults at different life-stages. There is no sense in which adult roles are portrayed as arbitrary or even oppressive, or that alternative roles and options are possible for a given life period. In this sense adult education contributes towards the maintenance of social norms and structures.

One need not look very far to find other instances of this type of approach. A significant example can be found in McCoy's tabulation of 'Adult life cycle tasks and educational program responses' which is reproduced in Chickering's influential volume The Modern American College. McCoy identifies seven developmental stages, each of which is characterized by a set of common tasks. For example, the 'leaving home' stage has the associated tasks of 'break psychological ties','choose career','enter work', 'manage time' and so on. Each stage is then related to an appropriate range of programme responses, with a final column indicating the outcomes sought from the educational re-programme. The table is too lengthy to reproduce here but a cross-section of one stage only will be sufficient to illustrate the general strategy. Table shows the 'tasks' and 'program responses' appropriate for the developmental stage 'becoming adult'.

Educational responses to life-cycle tasks

Task	*Programme responses*
1 Select mate	Marriage workshops
2 Settle in work, begin career ladder	Management, advancement training
3 Parent	Parenting workshops
4 Become involved in community	Civic education; volunteer training
5 Consume wisely	Consumer education; financial management training
6 Homo-own	Homo-owning, maintenance workshops

7 Socially interact	Human relations groups, translation analysis
8 Achieve autonomy	Living alone, divorce workshops
9 Problem-solve	Creative problem-solving workshops
10 Manage stress accompanying change	Stress management, biofeedback, relaxation, workshops

A casual glance at the list of tasks and how each of them relates to specified programmes confirms my general point about adult education supporting the status quo. Even a non-specific 'task' such as 'achieving autonomy', is interpreted in the most narrow sense possible - that is, as the capacity to 'live alone successfully'. It is unnecessary to elaborate further, the tabulation speaks for itself. What is surprising, and disappointing, is that anyone in adult education would take such an analysis seriously as anything other than a narrow descriptive exercise.

Yet there is a strongly held view among adult educators that the everyday reality of learners should be acknowledged, no matter how culturally specific that reality may be. The reader may remonstrate that McCoy is simply following this precept—what, then, is so objectionable? As I see it, there are two objections. The first of these is that there is no acknowledgement of the narrow culturally specific 'tasks' which are identified. Quite the opposite, the 'tasks' are presented as a generalizable framework to be used by adult education agencies in formulating their programmes. There is no sense in which McCoy is using her analysis as a case study of a process for others to emulate in a different cultural context. The second objection, already mentioned in relation to Knox, is that the response of adult education is depicted as solely adaptive. There is no scope for questioning and challenging the tasks - they constitute the taken for granted reality of the learners and the adult educators.

There are many adult educators who, being dismissive of the above approach, nevertheless subscribe to the view that adult development is a central concept in adult education. An interest in adult development stems quite naturally from a commitment to the notion of lifelong learning and the associated concepts of 'lifelong education', 'recurrent education' and '*education permanente*'. The policy and research documents of UNESCO, the OECD and the Council of Europe, which are the major sponsoring bodies of these concepts, frequently cite adult development as a central concern of any lifelong learning strategy. However, they do not understand adult development to be an immutable sequence of stages through which people pass at more or less predictable ages. Indeed, they challenge the concept of the 'typical' life cycle and support their view with an analysis of contemporary social and economic change. This is particularly apparent in the literature on recurrent education, and the following extract, taken from an article by one of its chief proponents, Jarl Bengtsson, typifies this approach:

Significant changes are taking place in the relationship between work and non-work time seen over the individual's whole life cycle in terms of increased education, earlier retirement, longer holidays, etc. It has also been made clear that these changes affect social groups according to their hierarchical position in working life, as well as the way their work is being scheduled, i.e. full-time, part-time, shift-work, long spells of employment, etc.

The claim is not that more non-work time is or will be used for education, although that certainly remains a strong possibility. Rather it is that to look at recurrent education from this perspective provides a very useful point of departure for placing it in the broader context of emerging new life-styles and life cycles. Most likely, the crucial factors behind changes in the individual's life-cycle pattern will be the economic and employment conditions that the industrialized countries will face during coming years.

Recurrent education, and its closely related concepts, accepts the diversity of life-cycle patterns and the need for educational institutions to respond to and foster this diversity through a diversity of provision. It supports the notion that individual options should be extended, especially the way in which paid work, education and leisure are combined. The principles espoused can be seen as a response to the effects of social, economic and technological change. Changes in demographic patterns, the sexual division of labour, the length of working life, hours spent at work, retirement age and so on, are all seen as relevant to the proposition that educational opportunities should be distributed, in a recurring way, across the life-span. Recurrent education also embodies the notion of social justice, and its evolution as a concept from the late 1960s has been linked with a host of terms implying broad social reforms: industrial democracy, participation in planning, social equity, decentralization, links between education and work and between younger and older generations, and concern with the disadvantaged. An underlying value in all this is a humanistic concern for the individual. The idea of self-development, which is based on notions of individuality and growth, is contrasted with the opposing notions of enslavement, alienation and stagnation—which are the psychological consequences of clinging to an outmoded conception of the 'normal' life cycle.

There are two persistent problems which are a feature of adult developmental psychology. The first is that there are insurmountable methodological difficulties in establishing 'phases' or 'stages' of adult life. The second is that much of the literature is historically and socially rooted and lacks any worthwhile generalizability.

Methodological difficulties

Not all adult development studies adopt a stage-sequence approach; nevertheless, they usually have a stake in making comparisons between different 'ages', 'phases' or 'stages' of life. Leaving aside the problem of deciding what type of data to gather, the common methodological problem is to construct a research design which generates comparative data. Many of the most influential studies in adult development use research design which fail to do this. Three basic research designs are the 'cross-sectional', 'longitudinal' and 'time-lag' designs. Perhaps the best known example of this technique is to be found in the research of Gould. In an initial study Gould observed and recorded the concerns expressed by a number of psychiatric outpatients. He hypothesized that these concerns differed among different age groups. He then used these expressed concerns to construct a questionnaire which contained 160 questions divided into ten areas of life. This questionnaire was then administered, in a later study, to a sample of 524 non-patients, who were white middle-class men and women aged 16-50 years.

The difficulty with a research design such as this is that the observed differences in 'concerns' may be due to the different life experiences of the different age cohorts. For example, the life history of a 5-year-old in 1972 would necessarily include the 'great depression' of the 1930s and the experience of the Second World War. This would be quite different from the life history of 22-year-old in 1972 who would have experienced the economic boom of the post-Second World War years and the social changes of the 1960s. It seems reasonable to assume that such historical events and trends affect people's 'concerns'. Indeed they may be more significant in explaining the different concerns of different age cohorts than any hypothesized notion of the life cycle.

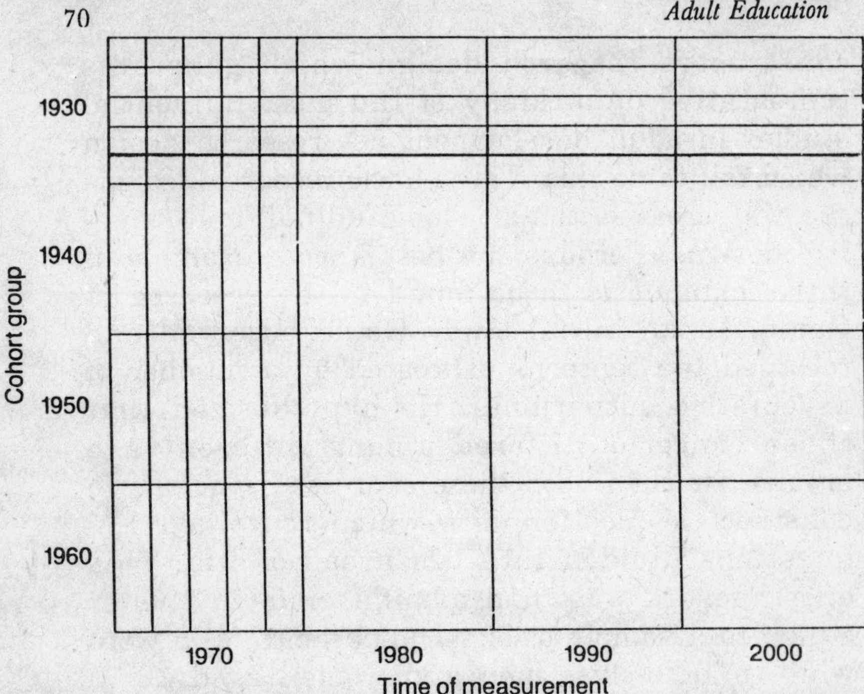

Adult development: basic research designs

One way to avoid making comparisons between different cohorts is to investigate a single age cohort over a number of years. Ninety-four college graduates from the early 1940s were followed through until 1969. They were part of an initial study of 268 male undergraduates who were given extensive physiological and psychological examinations early in their college years. After graduation the sample of 94 graduates completed annual questionnaires untitled 1955, and every two years after that date. They were interviewed in their homes twice, between 1950 and 1952 and in 1969. Vaillant reports the results in detail, but his thesis is simple: that ego defence mechanisms mature through the life cycle and that healthy adults progress through a hierarchy of adaptive mechanisms as shown in Table.

Hierarchy of adaptive mechanisms

Level I:	Psychotic mechanisms (common in psychosis, dreams, childhood)
	Denial (of external reality)
	Distortion
	Delusional projection
Level II:	Immature mechanisms (common in severe depression, personality disorders and adolescence)
	Fantasy (schizoid withdrawal, dental through fantasy)
	Projection
	Hypochondriasis
	Passive-aggressive behavior (masochism, turning against the self)
	Acting out (compulsive delinquency, perversion)
Lvel III:	Neurotic mechanisms (common in everyone)
	Intellectualization (isolation, obsessive behavior, undoing, rationalization)
	Repression
	Reaction formation
	Displacement (conversion, phobias, wit)
	Dissociation (neurotic denial)
Level IV:	Mature mechanisms (common in 'healthy' adults)
	Sublimation
	Altruism
	Suppression
	Anticipation
	Humor

There are some well-documented problems with long and practice effects and time-of-measurement effects. A significant problem, and one often overlooked, is that over, say, a 30 year period, there are bound to be shifts in the theoretical perspective of the theory upon which the research is based. This often means that the initial questions and modes of analysis become obsolescent and are replaced by more contemporary techniques. This certainly happened in Vaillant's study:

Unfortunately, the work of four other innovative students of personality in the 1930s was ignored. I say unfortunately because the work of these four men and women has affected my interpretation of the results of the Study. Erik Erikson, Anna Freud, Harry Stack Sullivan and Heinz Hartmen all significantly influenced modern understanding of personality; but in 1937-1942 their work was still too novel to shape the early design of the Grant Study.

By 1940 Harry Stack Sullivan had begun to revolutionize the psychodynamic theory of personality. Slowly, Sullivan and his British counterpart, Melanie Klein, led psychiatrists to realize that interpersonal, relations played as important a role in shaping personality as did the intrapersonal relations between ego, conscience and instinct, but not before the Grant Study was well under way. For example, although in college the psychiatric interviews had included a careful history of adolescent sexual development, the Study psychiatrists did not inquire into the boys' friendship patterns, or their efforts at heterosexual intimacy. Not until 1950, really, did the Grant Study begin to pay close attention to the men's relationships with older men and women.

In 1937 Anna Freud first published in English 'The Ego and The Mechanisms of Defense' and Heinz Hartmann had presented German 'Ego Psychology and the Problem of Adaptation'. Not until 1967 did the Grant Study focus on these men's styles of psychological adaptation.

In the late 1930s at the University of California Erikson had begun the work that in 1950 was to culminate in 'Childhood and Society'-providing convincing evidence that adults mature as well as children. During the same period, the Grant Study staff, like their colleagues elsewhere, saw psychodynamic maturation as being largely completed by adolescence.

Even though longitudinal studies overcome the problems of comparing different cohorts, they nevertheless remain historically bound. This means that generalizations to different cohort groups can only be made on the assumption that historical variation is unimportant.

Is it possible to avoid the influence of historical variation? The answer to this question rests heavily on one's analysis of how history and culture influence the psychological make-up of individuals. From a research design of view it is certainly possible to control for historical effects by using some combination of longitudinal and cross-sectional designs. Vertical columns in Figure would represent a cross-sectional sequence where all four cohort groups are investigated twice, once in 1970 and again in 1980. Similarly, combining the bottom two rows would represent a longitudinal sequence, where two cohort groups are investigated simultaneously over a number of years. Though such techniques it is possible to obtain data about the effects of cohort differences, time-of-easurement differences and age differences. For example, the differences between 20-year-olds can be compared with the differences between 30-year-olds in order to gauge the effect of cohort membership on the general difference between 20-and 30-year-olds. This, in effect, is a way of 'controlling' for historical variation. But the control gained through such a practice is very limited. First, it depends on whether the changes being monitored are easily quantifiable. In fact, most of the studies of this kind have been developed by those with an interest in measuring the development of human abilities, especially intellectual development. The research designs employed were initially intended to partial out the historical effects of improvements in educational provision during or between the lifetimes of the subjects being studied. This is easy to do when it is simply a matter of comparing test scores, but it is a dubious task to take such comparisons with qualitative data of the king found in adult personality development. Second, there is an assumption that the impact of histories linear and cumulative. But this is an untenable assumption.

Another way of minimizing the impact of historical variation on developmental research is to gather 'data' of a high level of generality. For example, Lowenthal et al. used a cross-sectional technique to investigate the adaptive processes of men and women across the life-span. In their study they documented such general psychological qualities as complexity, self-image, expressiveness and perceptions in continuity of value structure. The biographical interview technique of Levinson was primarily aimed at elucidating changes in the relationship between self and world throughout the life course. Loevinger was also concerned with the rather abstract notion of ego as a central frame of reference for understanding self and others. However, a closer look at this research will still reveal its social and historical specificity.

Social and historical bias

In the immediately preceding section on methodological difficulties I outlined some of the research design problems when comparing different people of different ages at a given time or when comparing the same people at different ages.

Unfortunately, research in adult development, especially the genre concerned with life 'stages' or 'phases', seems prone and historical bias. This is evident in four ways; the existence of purely descriptive inventories of life 'tasks', the selection of subjects for research, the data gathering techniques, and the way in which the concept of the 'healthy' personality is constructed.

Descriptive inventories

This approach, whereby an inventory of life tasks is constructed, has its origins in Havighurst's

Developmental Tasks and Education which was written in the early 1940s. It is similar to the inventory of McCoy and the same objections apply here. It is worthwhile noting, however, Havighurst's comments on his original inventory.

The tasks the individual must learn—the developmental task of life-are those things that constitute healthy and satisfactory growth in our society. They are the things a person must learn if he is to be judged and to judge himself to be a reasonably happy and successful person. A developmental task is a task which arises at or about a certain period in the life of the individual, successful achievement of which leads to his happiness and to success with later tasks, while failure leads to unhappiness in the individual, disapproval by the society, and difficulty with later tasks.

Thus the developmental tasks of life amount to a socially approved timetable for individual growth and development. In a pluralistic society this timetable will differ between social groups. While it may be useful to identify the developmental tasks of particular social or community groups, as Tucker and Huerta have done in their study of Mexican-American females, it is dangerous to generalize about the developmental tasks of society as such.

Sample selection, data gathering techniques

Table sets out the sample, method and developmental processes identified by each of six well-known adult developmental psychologists.

Five of these gathered data prior to formulating their views about adult development. An impressionistic description of the samples used is that they consisted of North American, white, middle class, better educated, predominantly male subjects.

The techniques for gathering data were the structured interview, questionnaire, self-rating checklist, standard psychological test and observer rating. But one should be wary of accepting reported results without a detailed knowledge of how these techniques were applied in each case.

Conceptions of the healthy personality

Development implies growth and progress, not merely change. But growth and progress towards what end? The answer to this question is often the starting point for theories of adult development, and it is the conception of the end point of development, the 'mature' or 'healthy' personality which frequently governs how progress and growth is monitored and explained within a given theory. Many developmental psychologists construe the end point of development with terms like 'individuality', 'autonomy' and the 'integrated self'.

But do such descriptions represent a particular way of looking at the world which excludes certain cultures or sections of the population? A closer look may help to resolve this issue. Levinson, for example, makes the following remarks about the 'individuation' prices:

Throughout the life cycle, but especially in the key transition periods such as infancy, pubescence and the Mid-life Transition, the developmental process of individuation is going on. This term refers to the changes in a person's relationship to himself and to the external world.

These changes are part of the individuation process. In successive periods of development, as this process goes on, the person forms a clearer boundary between self and world. He forms a stronger sense of who he is and what he wants, and a more realistic, sophisticated view of the world: what it is like, what it offers him and demands from him. Greater individuation allows him to be more separate from the world, to be more independent and self-generating. But it also gives him the confidence and understanding to have more intense attachments in the world and to feel more fully a part of it.

This emphasis on 'separateness', 'independence' and 'self-generation' is the language of the ethic of individualism, it is worthwhile noting the claims of at least one commentator, Gilligan, that the emphasis on the development of individual identity among developmental theories is an aspect of gender bias which pervades the literature. She begins her analysis by referring to the work of Chodorow, who observes that, in general, girls are parented by a person of the same gender while boys are parented by a person if the opposite gender. The significance of this is that the identity of boys is built on the perception of contrast and separateness from their primary caregiver, while the identity of girls is built upon the perception of sameness and attachment to their primary caregiver.

Consequently, relationships, and particularly issues of dependency, are experienced differently by women and men. For boys and men, separation and individuation are critically tied to gender identity since separation from the mother is essential for the development for masculinity. For girls and women, issues of feminity or feminine identity do not depend on the achievement of separation from the mother or on the progress of individuation. Since masculinity is defined through separation while femininity is defined through attachment, male gender identity is threatened by intimacy while female gender identity is threatened by separation. Thus males tend to have difficulty with relationships, while females tend to have problems with individuation. The quality of embeddedness in social interaction and personal relationships that characterizes women's lives in contrast to men's, however, becomes not only a descriptive difference but also a developmental liability when the milestones of childhood and adolescent development in the psychological literature are markets of increasing separation. Women's failure to separate then becomes by definition a failure to develop.

Gilligan then proceeds to cite evidence of the undervaluing of female characteristics—the concern with relationships and responsibilities, empathy and attachment-among developmental theories. For example, Freud considered the persistence of women's pre-Oedipal attachment to their mother to be linked with their failure to resolve completely their Oedipal feelings and their consequent failure to develop a strong superego. This developmental failure in women results in their having little sense of justice:

> The fact that women must be regarded as having little sense of justice is no doubt related to the predominance of envy in their mental life...

Another example comes from Jean Piaget, who observed sex differences in the way children engage in games. Girls, because of their more flexible attitude towards rules and their enforcement were considered to have a less developed legal sense than boys—which is the cornertone of corstone o moral development.

> The rule is no longer an imperative coming from an adult and accepted without discussion, it is a means of agreement resulting from co-operation itself. But girls are less explicit about this agreement and this is our reason for suspecting them of being less concerned with legal elaborations. A rule is good so long as the game repay it.

Kohlberg too is open to the same criticism. Gilligan observes that his empirical work, which led to the formulation of moral development stages, was based on a sample of boys only. According to Gilligan, this is because the higher stages of kohlberg's scale are constructed from what are traditionally 'male' qualities—the concern with justice and rights rather than with responsibilities and relationships.

The thrust of Gilligan's argument is that womanhood is rarely equated with mature healthy adulthood in much of the adult developmental literature. This is because the healthy personality is too often portrayed from a male perspective, with an emphasis on individuation and autonomy.

The elusive mystery of women's development lies in its recognition of the continuing importance of attachment in the human life cycle. Woman's place in man's life cycle is to protect this recognition while the developmental litany intones the celebration of separation, autonomy, individuation, and natural rights.

Development as a dialectical process

An alternative to documenting the 'stages' and 'phases' of adult life is to understand development as an ongoing dialectical process. The basic notion here is that there is a constant 'dialectic' between the changing or developing person and the changing or evolving society. That is, the person creates, and is created by the society in which he/she lives. Accompanying this notion is the rejection of those psychological approaches which search for stability, equilibrium and balance in the life course. The person is construed as a changing person in a changing world, and the dialectical approach is very much concerned with the dynamics of change:

The preference for an equilibrium model in the behavioral science has been as firmly established as has the preference for abstract traits or competencies. Without any debate it has been taken for granted that a state of balance, stability, and rest is more desirable than a state of upheaval, conflict and change. Thus we have always aimed for a psychology of satisfaction but not of excitement. This preference has found expression in balance theory, equilibrium theory, steady state theory, and indirectly in the theory of cognitive dissonance. With the possible exception for the latter, these interpretations fail to explore the fact that every change has to be explained by the process of imbalance which forms the basis for any movement. Once this pre-requisite is recognized, stability appears as a transitory condition in the stream of ceaseless changes.

One source of such change is the historical change in one's culture, the other source is the change associated with one's age-related social category. Such changes are primarily mediated through people interacting in everyday life -thus an investigation of developmental change will entail an analysis of common, everyday interactions and the dialogues contained in them.

Rriegel's position has much in common with Berger and Luckmann's exposition for how personal identity is shaped, maintained and transmitted within a given social order. Their analysis offers a powerful account of how personal identity is a social construction which, especially in a modern pluralistic society, is constantly open to change and transformation. What is meant by the proposition that personal identity is a social construction? Put simply, the idea is as follows:

1 We do not have biologically determined identities;

2 We are all born into a particular social world which has been constructed by humans;

3 We develop a notion of who we are from the way 'significant' others;

4 These 'significant' ohters represent the social world and mediate it to us.

5 We take on the roles and attitudes of significant others, internalize them and make them our own;

6 We extend our identification with significant others to an identification with society as whole: 'Only by virtue of this generalized identification does his own self-identification attain stability and continuity. He now has not only an identity vis-a vis this or that significant other, but an identity in general...'

Identity, as a social construction, needs to be maintained through social interaction. The routines of everyday life serve to confirm the reality of the world and our place in it. In particular, the language used in everyday conversations confirms for us the silent, taken-for-granted world that forms the foundation of our personal identity. In modern pluralistic society, however, there is a multiplicity of world views or realities. Because there is no common social reality there is no socially produced stable structure of personal identity. This means that achieving a stable personal identity in modern society becomes an individual, private enterprise. Moreover, the possibility of transforming one's identity is always present. Indeed, one could argue that many life events require a change or re-orientation of identity.

Berger and Luckmann maintain that any transformation of identity requires a process of re-socialization. In extreme cases, such as with religious conversion, there may be a complete dismantling of one's former identity. This would require the following:

1 Affiliation with the new community;

2 Segregation for the individual from the inhabitants of other 'worlds', especially those from the 'world' being left behind;

3 A reinterpretation of the old 'reality ' in terms of the new 'reality'

Each of these steps can be recognized as extreme versions of what happens to many adults as they develop new personal, family, work and leisure pursuits. The difference between this analysis and the life-span development literature is that transformation does not imply a move towards some state of maturity—it simply means change, not improvement. Also, there are no propositions about the regularity and predictability of change—only that personal identity is open to change, subject to the existence of a community of others who maintain the change through discourse in everyday life.

The idea of the malleability of personal identity is both a source of hope and an occasion for despair. Hope, because it means that change is always possible' despair, because it implies that a belief in the real, true, authentic self is a fanciful indulgence.

The studies cited in this chapter represent only a sampling of a rich and diverse field of enquiry. They were chosen to reveal some of the pitfalls in theory and research in adult development. Adult development is, in principle germane to anyone with an interest in adult education. Too often, however, people with an applied intent will latch on to an easily assimilated theory, one which clearly differentiates and orders the 'phases' or 'stages' of life and which advances an unambiguous account of the process and end point of development. Adult educators may find such theories useful but they need to be wary of the methodological and conceptual difficulties. They also need to be mindful of the impact such theories have on shaping and maintaining conventionally held views about what it means to be a mature, healthy adult.

4 Programme Development for Adults

Purposeful, enlightening, and personally significant discussion is not only possible without previously specified learning objectives, it actually requires that no such specifications be made. As Paterson cogently argues, to engage in the collaborative exploration and interpretation of individual experience is the most meaningful form of discussion for adults. But such discussion cannot be tied to previously determined objectives. It must be open and subject to continuous negotiation. Teachers and learners will often hold conflicting beliefs, values, and notions of importance. The most illuminating encounter is one in which these beliefs, values, and notions are externalized and subjected to collaborative analysis and in which participants are always ready to alter lines of inquiry on the basis of newly realized insights or interests.

Our sfinal criticism of previously defined objectives in programme development for adults concerns the question of unplanned, incidental learning. If we use the attainment of previously specified learning objectives as the evaluative criterion for judging the success of an educational effort then we must logically relegate unplanned, serendipitous, and incidental outcomes to a position of secondary importance. Indeed, we may consider such learning to have no real value at all. This idea, however, has provided so repugnant to some educational evaluators that a whole school of goal-free evaluation has developed as a counter to it. Here, we might simply note that several writers have questioned the idea that the only learning outcomes of any value are those that correspond to previously specified objectives. Apps points out that it is impossible for educators to anticipate all the learning that will result from participation in adult education classes. Jones declares that "the unintended consequences of a learning situation are often much more important than the original restrictive catechism of goals which invariably assumes an instrumental role for learning".

Some empirical support for the view that learners may perceive the unplanned outcomes of course participation to be of considerable significance is presented by Fodor. In her investigation of incidental learning occurring in structured educational experiences, she surveyed 246 adult accounting students in three different colleges. The study confirmed the ubiquity of incidentally learned information, skills, and attitudes in a set of circumstances designed for purposeful learning. Particularly important was the encouragement for such learning received from peers. Fodor advised adult teachers to arrange for informal interactions among peers as part of the course experience, to give greater attention to the cultivation of incidental learning in study skills courses, and to direct students to materials or resources that could help them develop independence and self-knowledge.

It is evident, then, that no programmer can predict the range of learning outcomes that are likely to arise from participation in one class session, let alone from membership in a course lasting several months. When the difficulties of trying to arrange learning outcomes for one adult are multiplied many times, the irrelevance of the predefined objectives approach for most programs becomes immediately apparent. That we still persist in using this approach to guide our program planning style irrespective of the nature of our clientele or our educational purposes is an extreme example of the "emperor's clothing" syndrome.

If, as programmers, we assume that the only valid learning is that which corresponds to some specific format we have previously arranged,then we are guilty of an unusually high degree of intellectual arrogance. Such arrogance is not uncommon, however. For example, if a learner leaves a programme before the end of the course, such withdrawal is almost always regarded as symptomatic or failure—failure by the learner who did not apply his or her talents with sufficient industry or failure by the teacher who possessed inadequate pedagogic skills. An equally plausible interpretation, however, is that the learner feels that she has gained what was most valuable from the course and decides that, with limited time at her disposal, she would be better advised to pursue other avenues of learning. Indeed, withdrawal might sometimes be interpreted as a sign of the success of the course in that it has so animated a learner's interest in a field that she commits herself to a sustained and independent exploration of its boundaries.

It is timely to remind ourselves, then, that we cannot prescribe for our diverse clienteles the exact range, from, and number of learning outcomes that will result from their participation in our programmes. Learners' perceptions of what valuable learning may bear little relation to the previously determined objectives that we prescribe to determine instructional design, course content, and evaluative procedures. Learners will frequently take from course participation various skills, insights, and information that have nothing to do with the activities and outcomes initially intended by the educator.

In every learning group there may well be an optimal balance that can be attained among facilitators' purposes, participants' expectations, flexibility of format, and sense of overall direction. In the most satisfying of group transactions, this balance will be negotiated continually. This, of course, is not to advocate an abandonment of the concept of educational purpose, whether this be expressed in broad philosophical aims or in terms of specific behavioral or other performance objectives. Although various encounter or support groups may decide to meet for no other reason than to make contact with others of similar outlook and may be able to spend a great deal of time negotiating purposes, for many learning groups this will not be realistic. Community action groups, engaged in advocacy, work-study groups seeking to acquire occupational skills, and groups meeting to undertake hard intellectual analysis will most likely not wish to spend more than a small part of their time engaged in an initial negotiation of purpose. They will probably benefit from a regular formative evaluation session, in which progress is discussed and fundamental purposes reiterated, but the majority of participants' time will be spent in purposeful learning.

The point is, however, that incidental learning, unplanned acquisition of skills and knowledge, or unanticipated insights should not be regarded by participants or facilitators as somehow innately less valid than previously specified learning outcomes. A sense of common purpose is probably a precondition of effective group interaction and development of a moral culture within group. But it should not become reified to such an extent that deviations from the previously agreed-upon purpose are condemned as irrelevant even before they occur. This, in effect, may block off fruitful avenues of intellectual exploration and act against participants' making meaningful connections between learning activities and their own experiences.

The last comments on this question behavioral objectives might profitably be left to Eisner. As he remarks, "In thousands of ways, teachers draw on images of human virtue as criteria for the direction of their activity as teachers and for the directions they should take with their students. The storehouse of such images is large, and it needs to be. It is modulated according to the circumstances and context and with regard to the particular student with whom the teacher interacts". Why, then, should we regard it as unprofessional or irresponsible for facilitators to encourage learners to explore feelings, perceptions, and avenues of inquiry that were not originally specified as part of the learning group's activities? Arguably, the most exiting, memorable, and profound moments in learning are those in which individuals stumble into insights and perceptions of which they had previously been unaware .Such moments can rarely be planned beforehand in precise terms, though the facilitator can encourage a learning group culture that will make the likelihood of such moments occurring much stronger. A facilitator who can make unexpected connections between participants' contributions or who encourages learners to depart from the "script" of the sessions's activities to explore themes that were unanticipated but that engage and excite is the most valuable.

The needs revealed by a needs assessment are what provide the goals an daims of the programme, which are then translated into specific objectives curricula, and evaluative criteria. Griffith, however, has called the concept of need an adult education shibboleth in that the favored answer to questions concerning the function of an educational programme is that isit is meeting learners' needs, meeting adults needs or meeting the needs of the community

The concept of need also functions as a "premature ultimate" in discussions concerning the proper role of education and training programmes. A premature ultimate is a concept or term that provokes such reverence and contains such cannective potency that its invocation tends to silence any further discussion on a matter. Lawson points out that the term need functions in this manner when question concerning the curricula of training and education programmes are raised. Hence, to say that one is meeting needs in a programmes is to state a case rather than to argue a viewpoint. Discussion on the merits of the case comes to be seen as inappropriate. But to say that as a programmer one is meeting needs is somewhat akin to politicians saying that an action or policy is democratic. In both instances the justification invoked for the decisions taken is ambiguous, while at the same time it forecloses further discussion. What is important to realize is that many different interpretations can be made of the concept of need and that the concept is irrevocably value laden.

The value-laden aspect of the concept has been discussed in several analyses. As these writers all recognize, those who invoke the concept of need to justify their decisions should specify whether the needs in question are felt by learners or prescribed by educators. It is unpardonable to confuse the two, yet such confusion is frequently evident in the writings and conversations of educators and trainers. The difference between felt needs and prescribed needs has been discussed by the writers cited above and also by this writer. Felt needs are equivalent to the wants, desires, and wishes of the learner. They are perceived and expressed by the learners themselves. Examples of commonly felt needs of adult learners might be how to use microcomputers, how to lose weight through aerobics, how to speak a foreign language, or how to cook in a certain style. Prescribed needs arise when an educator decides that an individual, group, or community falls short of some ideal identified by that educator. Monette calls such a need a normative need that entails three propositions on the part of the educator: "that someone is in a given state, that this state is incompatible with the norms held by some group or by society, and that therefore the state of that someone should be changed".

Felt needs, then, are expressions of preference or desire by learners. Prescribed needs are premised upon educators' beliefs concerning the skills, knowledge, behaviors, and values that they feel adults should acquire. To base education and training programmes on a mix of felt and prescribed needs causes some educators to feel uncomfortable. It seems arrogant and authoritarian compared to the apparently democratic process of responding solely to the felt needs of learners. Nonetheless, it is my contention that a total subscription to a felt needs approach to programme development condemns education to an adaptive, reactive mode and turns educators into mere providers of consumer goods. The exact form of these goods, according to this rationale, is to be determined by the market forces of expressed learner preferences. The educator becomes an automation of functionary, a technician responding to expressed desires but with no responsibility for suggesting alternative curricula or activities. Such a view absolves the educator from ever having to make value choices or from having to prompt learners to consider the possibility of other ways of thinking, feeling, and behaving. This is entirely unacceptable as a way of viewing an educator's professional responsibilities. Those who behave in this manner and who equate the sum total of education with reacting to expressed learner needs are technicians, not educators.

The element of felt needs will determine some of the courses offered in every programme. It would be hard for educators and trainers of adults to survive in most institutional settings if their programmes did not clearly satisfy the felt needs of a reasonably large number of adults in the vicinity. Programmes will frequently be mounted to attract large numbers of participants so as to allow programmers to engage in educationally crucial but economically unviable work. For example, the price of my running a free Educational Advisory Service for adults in the community was my arranging courses on popular subjects. The service was established to assist adults in charting a path through the bewildering range of formal educational opportunities open to them and to discuss general learning difficulties they were experiencing in their intellectual pursuits. No fee was paid for this service, and it was open to adult who were not enrolled in courses at my center, as well as those who were. Courses on yoga or on Vegetarian Cooking attracted large numbers of participants and made it easier for me to argue that the Educational Advisory Service should be continued, despite its not generating revenue for the college, since this was offset by the fees collected from yoga and cooking classes.

The danger, however, is that courses dictated by the felt needs rationale will come to comprise the total programme offering. If this happens, then the programmer will be discouraged from engaging in provocative, controversial, or unpopular alternative programming. Encouraging adults to consider alternative ways of conceiving their world and acting within and upon it often involves a painful readjustment of perceptions. It is a threatening and traumatic experience to be prompted to reinterpret on's dearly held belief systems, value frameworks, and common behaviors from another perspective. We often bridle against being asked to consider the possibility that we might be operating under false assumptions or ignoring important realities.

A practical example may illustrate may point. It is my firm relief that every publicly funded adult education programme should sponsor some kind of political discourse, whether by setting up a formal course or by providing resources for groups already engaged in such activity in the community.

5 The Process of Experiential Learning

Experiential learning theory offers a fundamentally different view of the learning process from that of the behavioral theories of learning based on an empirical epistemology or the more implicit theories of learning that underlie traditional educational methods that for the most part are based on a rational, idealist epistemology. From this different perspective emerge some very different prescriptions for the conduct of education, the proper relationships among learning, worm, and other life activities, and the creation of knowledge itself.

This perspective on learning is called 'experimental' for two reasons. The first is to tie it clearly to its intellectual origins in the work of Dewey, Lewin, and Piaget. Then second reason is to emphasize the central role that experience plays in the learning process. This differentiates experiential that tend to give primary emphasis to acquisition, manipulation, and recall of abstract symbols, and from behavioral learning theories that deny any role for consciousness and subjective experience in the learning process. It should be emphasized, however, the aim is not to pose experiential learning theory as a third alternative to behavioral and cognitive learning theories, but rather to suggest through experiential learning theory a holistic integrative perspective on learning that combines experience, perception, cognition, and behaviour. This chapter will describe the learning models of Lewin, Dewey, and Piaget and identify the common characteristics they share—characteristics that serve to define the nature of experiential learning.

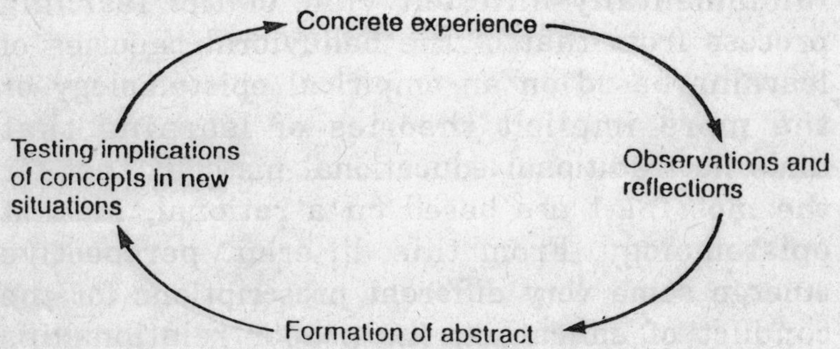

The Lewinian experiential learning model

Three models of the experiential learning process

The Lewinian model of action research and laboratory training

In the techniques of action research and the laboratory method, learning change, and growth are seen to be facilitated best by an integrated process that begins with here-and-now experience followed by collection of data and observations about that experience. The data are then analyzed and the conclusions of this analysis are fed back to the actors in the experience for their use in the modification of their behaviour and choice of new experiences. Learning is thus conceived as a four-stage cycle. Immediate concrete experience is the basis for observation and reflection. These observations are assimilated into a 'theory' from which new implications for action can be deduced. These implications or hypotheses then serve as guides in acting to create new experiences.

Two aspects of this learning model are particularly noteworthy. First is its emphasis on here-and-now concrete experience to validate and test abstract concepts. Immediate personal experience is the focal point for learning, giving life, texture, and subjective personal meaning to abstract concepts and at the same time providing a concrete, publicly shared reference point for testing the implications and validity of ideas created during the learning process. When human beings share an experience, they can share it fully, concretely, and abstractly.

Second, action research and laboratory training are based on feedback processes. Lewin borrowed the concept of feedback from electrical engineering to describe a social learning and problem-solving process that generates valid information to assess deviations from desired goals. This information feedback provides the basis for a continuous process of goal-directed action and evaluation of the consequences of that action. Lewin and his followers believed that much individual and organizational ineffectiveness could be traced ultimately to a lack of adequate feedback processes. This ineffectiveness results from an imbalance between observation and action - either from a tendency for individuals and organizations to emphasize decision and action at the expense of information gathering, or from a tendency to become bogged down by data collection and analysis. The aim of the laboratory method and action research is to integrate these two perspectives into an effective, goal-directed learning process.

Dewey's model of learning

John Dewey's model of the learning process is remarkably similar to the Lewinian model, although he makes more explicit the developmental nature of learning implied in Lewin's conception of it as a feedback process by describing how learning transforms the impulses, feelings, and desires of concrete experience into higher-order purposeful action.

The formation of purposes is, then, a rather complex intellectual operation. It involves: (1) observation of surrounding conditions; (2) knowledge of what as happened in similarity situations in the past, a knowledge obtained partly by recollection and partly from the information, advice, and warning of those who have had a wider experience; and (3) judgment, which puts together what is observed and what is recalled to see what they signify. A purpose differs from an original impulse and desire through its translation into a plan and method of action based upon foresight of the consequences of action under given observed conditions in a certain way... The crucial educational problem is that of procuring the postponement of immediate action upon desire until observation and judgment have intervened...Mere foresight, even if it takes the form of accurate prediction, is not, of course, enough. The intellectual anticipation, the idea of consequences, must blend with desire and impulse to acquire moving force. It then gives direction to what otherwise is blind, while desire gives ideas impetus and momentum.

Dewey's model of experiential learning is graphically portrayed. We note in his description of learning a similarity with Lewin, in the emphasis on learning as a dialectic process integrating experience and concepts, observation, and action. The impulse of experience gives ideas their moving force, and ideas give direction to impulse. Postponement of immediate action is essential for observation and judgment to intervene, and action is essential for achievement of purpose. It is through the integration of these opposing but symbiotically related processes that sophisticated, mature purpose develops from blind impulse.

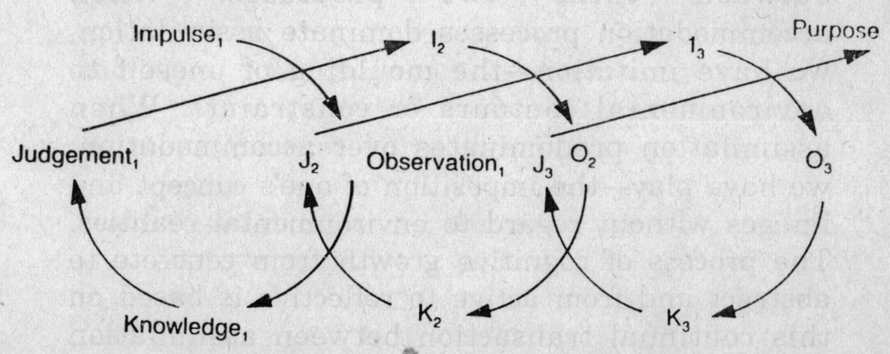

Dewey's model of experiential learning

Piaget's model of learning and cognitive development

For Piaget, the dimensions of experience and concept, reflection, and action form the basic continua for the development of adult thought. Development from infancy to adulthood moves from a concrete phenomenal view of the world to an abstract constructionist view, from an active egocentric view to a reflective internalized mode of knowing. Piaget also maintained that these have been the major directions of development in scientific knowledge. The learning process whereby this development takes place is a cycle of interaction between the individual and the environment that is similar to the learning models of Dewey and Lewin. In Piaget's terms, the key to learning lies in the mutual interaction of the process of accommodation of concepts or schemes to experience in the world and the process of assimilation of events and experiences from the world into existing concepts and schemes. Learning or, in Piaget's term, intelligent adaptation results from a balanced tension between these two processes. When accommodation processes dominate assimilation, we have imitation—the moulding of oneself to environmental contours or constraints. When assimilation predominates over accommodation, we have play—the imposition of one's concept and images without regard to environmental realities. The process of cognitive growth from concrete to abstract and from active to reflective is based on this continual transaction between assimilation and accommodation, occurring in successive stages, each of which incorporates what has gone before into a new, higher level of cognitive functioning.

Piaget's work has identified four major stages of cognitive growth that emerge from birth to about the age of 14-16. In the first stage the child is predominantly concrete and active in his learning style. This stage is called the sensory-motor stage. Learning is predominantly through feeling, touching, and handling. Representation is based on action - for example, 'a hole is to dig'. Perhaps the greatest accomplishment of this period is the development of goal-oriented behaviour: "The sensory-motor period shows a remarkable evolution from non-intentional habits to experimental and exploratory activity which is obviously intentional orgoal oriented'. Yet the child has few schemes or theories into which he can assimilate events, and as a result, his primary stance towards the world is accommodative. Environment plays a major role in shaping his ideas and intentions. Learning occurs primarily through the association between stimulus and response.

In the second stage, the child retains his concrete orientation but begins to develop a reflective orientation as he begins to internalize actions, converting them to images. This is called the representational stage. Learning is now predominantly iconic in nature, through the manipulation observations and images. he child is new freed somewhat from his immersion in immediate experience and as a result, is free to play with and manipulate his images of the world.

At this stage, the childs primary stance towards the world is divergent. He is captivated with his ability to collect images and to view the world from different perspectives.

In the third stage, the intensive development of abstract symbolic powers begins. The first symbolic developmental stage Piaget calls the stage of concrete operations. Learning in this stage is governed by the logic of classes and relations. The child in this stage further increases his independence from his immediate experiential world through the development of inductive powers. Thus, in contrast to the child in the sensory-motor stage whose learning style was dominated by accommodative processes, the child at the stage of concrete operations is more assimilative in his learning style. He relies on concepts and theories to select and give shape to his experiences.

Piaget's final stage of cognitive development comes with the onset of adolescence. In this stage, the adolescent moves from symbolic processes based on concrete operations to the symbolic processes of representational logic, the stage of formal operations. He now returns to a more active orientation, but it is an active orientation that is now modified by the development of the reflective and abstract power that preceded it. The symbolic powers he now possesses enable him to engage in hypothetico-deductive reasoning. He develops the possible implications of his theories and proceeds to experimentally test which of these are true. Thus his basic learning style is convergent, in contrast to the divergent orientation of the child in the representational stag. This brief outline off Piaget's cognitive development theory identifies those basic developmental processes that shape the basic learning process of adults.

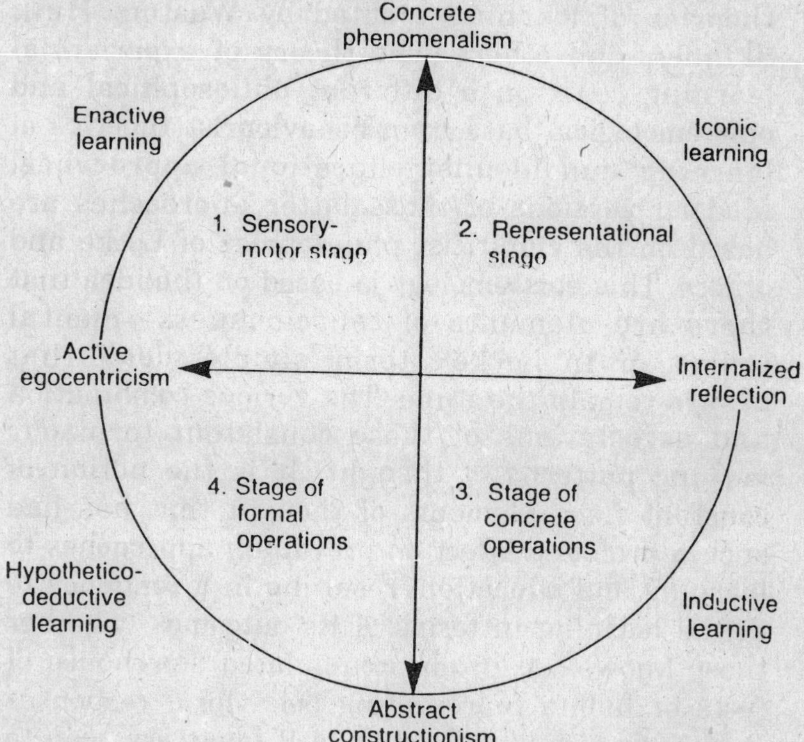

Piagets, Model of learning and cognitive development

Characteristics of experiential learning

There is a great deal of similarity among the models of the learning process discussed above. Taken together, they form a unique perspective on learning and development, a perspective that can be characterized by the following propositions, which are shared by the three major traditions of experiential learning.

Learning is best conceived as a process, not in terms of outcomes

The emphasis on the process of learning as opposed to the behavioral outcomes distinguishes experiential learning from the idealist approaches of traditional education and from the behavioral theories of learning created by Waston, Hull, Skinner, and others. The theory of experiential learning rests on a different philosophical and epistemological base from behaviourist theories of learning and idealist educational approaches. Modern versions of these latter approaches are based on the empiricist philosophies of Locke and others. This epistemology is based on the idea that there are elements of consciousness—mental atoms, or in Locke's term 'simple idea'—that always remain the same. The various combination and associations of these consistent form our varying patterns of thought. It is the notion of constant fixed elements of thought that has had such a profound effect on prevailing approaches to learning and education, resulting in a tendency to define learning in terms of its outcomes, whether these knowledge in an accumulated storehouse of facts or habits representing behavioral responses to specific stimulus conditions If ideas are seen to be fixed and immutable, then it seems possible to measure how much someone has learned by the amount of these fixed ideas the person has accumulated

Experiential learning theory, however, proceeds from a different set of assumptions. Ideas are not fixed and immutable elements of thought but are formed and re-formed through experience. In all three of the leaning models just reviewed, learning is described as a process whereby concepts are derived from, and continuously modified by experience. No two thoughts are ever the same, since experience always intervenes. Learning is an emergent process whose outcomes represent only historical record, not knowledge of the future.

When viewed from the perspective of experiential learning, the tendency to define learning in terms of outcomes can become a definition of nonlearning, in the process sense that the failure to modify ideas and habits as a result of experience is maladaptive. The clearest example of this irony lies in the behaviorist axiom that the strength of a habit can be measured by its resistance to extinction. That is, the more I have 'learned' a given habit, the longer I will persist in behaving that way when it is no longer rewarded. Similarly, there are those who feel that the orientations that conceive of learning in terms of outcomes as opposed to a process of adaptation have had a negative effect on the education system. Jerome Bruner, in his influential book, Toward a Theory of Instruction, makes the point that the purpose of education is to stimulate enquiry and skill in the process of knowledge getting, not to remorize a body of knowledge: 'Knowing is a process, not a product'. Paulo Freire calls the orientation that conceives of education as the transmission of fixed content the 'banking' concept of education:

Education thus becomes an act of depositing, in which the students are the depositories and the teacher is the depositor. Instead of communicating, the teacher issues communiques and makes deposits which the students patiently receive, memorize, and repeat. This is the 'banking' concept of education, in which the scope of action allowed to the students extends only as far as receiving filing and storing the deposits. They do, it is true, have the opportunity to become collectors or cateloguers of the things they store. But in the last analysis, it is men themselves who are filed away through the lack of creativity, transformation, and knowledge in this misguided system. For apart from inquiry, apart from the praxis, men cannot be truly human. Knowledge emerges only through invention and reinvention, through the restless, impatient, continuing, hopeful inquiry men pursue in the world, with the world, and with each other.

Learning is a continuous process grounded in experience

Knowledge is continuously derived from and tested out in the experiences of the learner. William James, in his studies on the nature of human consciousness, marvelled at the fact that consciousness is continuous. How is it, he asked, that is awake in the morning with the same consciousness, the same thoughts, feelings, memories, and sense of who I that I went to sleep with the night before? Similarly for Dewey, continuity of experience was a powerful truth of human existence, central to the theory of learning: 'the principle of continuity of experience means that every experience both takes up something from those which have gone before and modifies in some way the quality of those which come after.

Although we are all aware of the sense of continuity in consciousness and experience to which James and Dewey refer, and take comfort from the predictability and security it provides, there is no occasion in the penumbra of that awareness an element of doubt and uncertainty. How do I reconcile my own sense of continuity and predictability with what at times appears to be a chaotic and unpredictable world around me? I move through my daily round of tasks and meetings with a fair sense of what the issues are, of what others are saying and thinking, and with ideas about what actions to take. Yet I am occasionally upended by unforeseen circumstances, miscommunications. and dreadful miscalculations. It is in this interplay between expectation and experience that learning occurs.

The fact that learning is a continuous process grounded in experience has important educational implications. Put simply, it implies that all learning is relearning. How easy and tempting it is in designing a course to think of the learner's mind as being as blank as the paper on which we scratch our outline. Yet this is not the case. Every one enters every learning situation with more or less articulate ideas about the topic at hand. We are all psychologists, historians, and atomic physicists. It is just that some of our theories are more crude and incorrect than others. But to focus solely on the refinement and validity of these theories misses the point. The important point is that the people we teach have held these beliefs whatever their quality and that until now they have used them whenever the situation called for them to be atomic physicists, historians or whatever.

Thus, one's job as an educator is not only to implant new ideas but also to dispose of or modify old ones. In many cases, resistance to new ideas stems from their conflict with old beliefs that are inconsistent with them. If the education process begins by bringing out the learners beliefs and theories, examining and testing them, and then integrating the new, more refined ideas into the person's belief systems, the learning process will be facilitated. Piaget has identified two mechanisms by which new ideas are adopted by an individual—integration and substitution. Ideas that evolve through intergration tend to become highly stable parts of the person's conception of the world. On the other hand, when the content of a concept changes by means of substitution, there is always the possibility of a reversion to the earlier level of conceptualization and understanding, or to a dual theory of the world where espoused theories learned through substitution are incongruent with theories-in-use that are more integrated with the person's total conceptual and attitudinal view of the world. It is this latter outcome that stimulated Argyris and Schon's inquiry into the effectiveness of professional education:

We thought the trouble people have in

learning new theories may stem not so much from the inherent difficulty of the new theories as from the existing theories people have that already determine practices. We call their operational theories of action Theories-in-use to distinguish them from the espoused theories that are used to describe and justify behavior. We wondered whether the difficulty in learning new theories of action is related to a disposition to protect the old theory-in-use.

Resolution of conflicts between dialectically opposed modes of adaptation to the world

Each of the three models of experiential learning describes conflicts between opposing ways of dealing with the world, suggesting that learning results from resolution of these conflicts. The Lewinian model emphasizes two such dialectics-the conflict between concrete experience and abstract concepts and the conflict between observation and action. For Dewey, the major dialectic is between the impulse that gives ideas their 'moving force' and reason that gives desire its direction. In Piaget's framework, the twin processes of accommodation of ideas to the external world and assimilation of experience into existing conceptual structures are the moving forces of cognitive development. In Paulo Freire's work, the dialectic nature of learning and adaptation is encompassed in his concept of praxis, which he defines as "reflection and action upon the world in order to transform it'. Central to the concept of praxis is the process of naming the world', which is both active and reflective. This process of naming the world is accomplished through dialogue among equals, a joint process of inquiry and learning that Freire sets against the banking concept of education described earlier:

> As we attempt to analyze dialogue as a human phenomenon, we discover something which is the essence of dialogue itself: the word. But the word is more than just an instrument which makes dialogue possible accordingly, we must seek its constitutive elements. Within the word we find two dimensions, reflection and action, in such radical interaction that if one is sacrificed - even in part—the other immediately suffers. There is no true word that is not at the same time a praxis. Thus, to speak a true word is to transform the world.
>
> On the other hand, if action is emphasized exclusively, to the detriment of reflection, the word is converted into activism. The latter—action for action's sake—negates the true prraxis and makes dialogue impossible. Either dichotomy, by creating unauthentic forms of existence, creates also unauthentic forms of thought, which reinforce the original dichotomy.
>
> Human existence cannot be silent, nor can it be nourished by false words, but only by true words, with which men transform the world. To exist, humanly, is to name the world, to change it. Once named, the world in its turn appears to the namers as a problem and requires of them a new naming. Men are not built in silence, but in word, in work, in action-reflection.

But while to say the true word - which is work, which is praxis—is to transform the world, saying that word is not the priviege of some few men, but the right of every man. Consequently, no one can say a true word alone—nor can he say it for another, in a prescriptive act which robs others of their words.

All the models above suggest the idea that learning is by its very nature tension—and conflict-filled process. New knowledge, skills, or attitudes are achieved through confrontation among four modes of Yet this ideal is difficult to achieve. How can one act and reflect at the same time? How can one be concrete and immediate and still be theoretical? Learning requires abilities that are polar opposites, and the learner, as a result, must continually choose which set of leaning abilities he or she will bring to bear in any specific learning situation. More specifically, there are two primary dimensions to the learning process. The first dimension represents the concrete expriencing of events at one end and abstract conceptualization at the other. The other dimension has active experimentation at one extreme and reflective observation at the other. Thus, in the process of learning, one moves in varying degrees from actor to observer and from specific involvement to general analytic detachment.

In addition, the way in which the conflict among the dialectically opposed modes of adaptation get resolved determines the level of learning that results. If conflicts are resolved by suppression of one mode and/or dominance by another, learning tends to be specialized around the dominant mode and limited in areas controlled by the dominated mode. For example, in Piaget's model, imitation is the result when accommodation processes dominate, and play results when assimilation dominates. Or for Freire, dominance of the active mode results in 'activism', and dominance of the reflective mode results in verbalism'.

Learning is an holistic process of adaptation to the world

Experiential learning is not molecular educational concept but rather is a molar concept describing the central process of human adaptation to the social and physical environment. It is a holistic concept much akin to the Jungain theory of psychological types, in that it seeks to describe the emergence of basic life orientations as a function of dialectic tensions between basic modes of relating to the world. To learn is not the special province of a single specialized realm of human functioning of the total organism—thinking, feeling, perceiving, and behaving.

Learning is the major process of human adaptation. This concept of learning is considerably broader than that commonly associated with the school classroom. It occurs in all human settings, from schools to the workplace, from the research laboratory to the management board room, in personal relationshps and the aisles of the local grocery. We encompasses all life-stages, from childhood to adolescence, to middle and old age. Therefore it encompasses other, more limited adaptive concepts such as creativity, problem-solving, decision-making, and attitude change that focus heavily on one or another of the basic aspects of adaptation. Thus, creativity research has tended to focus on the divergent factors in adaption such as tolerance for ambiguity, metaphorical thinking, and flexibility, 3whereas research on decision-making has emphasized more couvergent adaptive factors such as the rational evaluation of solution alternatives.

The cyclic descriptions of the experiential learning process is mirrored in many of the specialized modes of the adaptive process. The common theme in all these models is that all forms of human adaptation approximate scientific inquiry, a point of view articulated most thoroughly by the late George Kelly. Dewey, Lewin, and Piagets in one way or another seem to take the scientific method as their model for the learning process; or to put it another way, they see in the scientific method the hightest philosophical and technological refinement of the basic processes of human adaptation. The scientific method, thus, provides a means for describing the holistic integration of all human functions.

The experiential learning cycle in the centre circle and a model of the scientific inquiry process in the outer circle, with models of the problem solving process, the decision making process, and the creative process in between. Although the models all use different terms, there is remarkable similarity in concept among them. This similarity suggests that there may be great payoff in the integration of findings from these specialized areas into a single general adaptive model such as that proposed by experiential learning theory. Burner's work on a theory of instruction shows one example of this potential payoff. His integration of research on cognitive processes, problem-solving, and learning theory provided a rich new perspective for the conduct of education.

When learning is conceived as a holistic adaptive process, it provides conceptual bridges across life situations such as school and work, portraying learning as a continuous, lifelong process. Similarly, this perspective highlights the similarities among adaptive/learning activities that are commonly called by specialized nemes - learning conceived holistically includes adaptive activities, that vary in their extension through time and space. Typically, an immediate reaction to a limited situation or problem is not thought of as learning but as performance. Similarly at the other extreme, we do not commonly think of long-term adaptations to one's total life situation as learning but as development. Performance is limited to short-term adaptations to immediate circumstance, learning encompasses somewhat longer-term mastery of generic classes of situations, and development encompasses lifelong adaptations to one's total life situation.

Learning involves transactions between the person and the environment

So stated, this proposition must seem obvious. Yet

strangely enough, its implication seem to have been widely ignored in research on learning and practice in education, replaced instead by a person-centred psychological view of learning. The casual observer of the traditional educational process would undoubtedly conclude that learning was primarily a personal, internal process requiring only the limited environment of books, teacher, and classroom. Indeed, the wider 'real-world' environment at times seems to be actively rejected by educational systems at all levels.

There is an analogous situation in psychological research on learning and development. In theory, stimulus-response theories of learning describe relationship between environmental stimuli and responses of the organism. But in practice, most of this research involves treating the environmental stimuli as independent variables manipulated artificially by the experimenter to determine their effect on dependent response characteristics. This approach has had two outcomes. The first is a tendency to perceive the person-environment relationship as one-way, placing great emphasis on how environment shapes behaviour with little regard for how behaviour shapes the environment. Second, the models of learning are essentially decontextualized and lacking in what Egon Brunswick called ecological validity. In the emphasis on scientific control of environmental conditions, laboratory situations were created that bore little resemblance to the environment of real life, resulting in empirically validated models of learning that accurately described behaviour in these artificial settings but could not easily be generalized to subjects in their natural environment.

Similar criticisms have been made of developmental psychology. Piaget's work, for example, has been criticized for its failure to take account of environmental and cultural circumstances. Speaking of developmental psychology in general. Bronfenbrenner states, 'Much of developmental psychology as it now exists is the science of the strange behavior of children in strange situations with strange adults for the briefest possible periods of time'.

In experiential learning theory, the transactional relationship—between the person and the environment is symbolized in the dual meanings of the term experience—one subjective and personal, referring to the person's internal state, as in the experience of joy and happiness', and the other objective and environmental, as in , 'He has 20 years of experiences on this job.' These two forms of experience interpenetrate and interrelate in very complex way, as, for example, in the old saw, ' He doesn't have 20 years of experience, but one year repeated 20 times.' Deway describes the matter this way:

Experience does not go on simply inside a person. It does go on there, for it influences the formation of attitudes of desire and purpose. But this is not the whole of the story. Every genuine experience has an active side which changes in some degree the objective conditions under which experience are had. The difference between civilization and savagery, to take an example on a large scale, is found in the degree in which previous experiences have changed the objective conditions under which subsequent experiences take place. The existence of roads, of means of rapid movement and transportation, tools, implements, furniture, electric light and power, are illustrations.

The word 'interaction' assigns equal rights to noth factors in experience - objective and internal conditions. Any normal experience is an interplay of these two sets of conditions. Taken together... they form what we call a situation.

The statement that individuals live in a world means, in the concrete, that they live in a series of situations. And when it is said that theyt live in these situations, the meaning of the word 'in' is different from its meaning when it is said that pennies are 'in' a pocket or paint is 'in' a can. It means, once more, that interaction is going on between an individual and objects and other persons. The conceptions of situation and of interaction are inseparable from each other. An experience is always what it is because of a transaction taking place between an individual and what, at the time, constitutes his environment, whether the latter consists of persons with whom he is talking about some topic or event, the subject talked about being also a part of the situation; the book he is reading; or the materials of an experiment is performing. The environment, in other words is whatever conditions interact with personal needs, desires, purposes, and capacities to create the experience which is had. Even when a person builds a castle in the air he is interacting which the objects he constructs in fancy.

Although Dewey refers to the relationship beteween the objective and subjective conditions of experience as an 'interaction', he is struggling in the last portion of the quote above to convey the special, complex nature of the relationship. The word transaction is more appropriate than interaction to describe the relationship between the person and the environment in experiential learning theory, because the connotation of interaction is somehow too mechanical involving unchanging separate entities that become intertwined but retain their seperate identities. This is why Dewey attempts to give special meaning to the word in. The concept of transaction mplies a more fluid, interpenetrating relationship between objective conditions and subjective experience, such that once they become related, both are essentially changed.

Learning is the process of creating knowledge

To understand learning, we must understand the nature and forms of human knowledge and the proces whereby this knowledge is created. It has already been emphasized that this process of creation occurs at all levels of sophistication, from the cost advanced forms of scientific research to the child's discovery that a rubber ball bounces.

Knowledge is the result of the transaction between social knowledge and personal knowledge. The former, as Dewey noted, is the civilized objective accumulation of previous human cultural experience, whereas the latter is the accumulation of the individual person's subjective life experiences. Knowledge results from the transaction between these objective and subjective experiences in a process called learning. Hence, to understand knowledge, we must understand the psychology of the learning process. and to understand learning, we must understand epistemology- the origins, nature, methods, and limits of knowledge.

It is surprising that few learning and cognitive researchers other than Piaget have recognized the intimate relationship between learning and knowledge and hence recognized the need for epistemological as well as psychological inquiry into these related processes. In my own research and practice with experiential learning, I have been impressed with the very practical ramification of the epistemological perspective. In teaching, for example, we have found it essential to take into account the nature of the subject matter in deciding how to help students learn the material at hand. Trying to develop skills in empathic listening is a different educational task, requiring a different teaching approach from that of teaching fundamental of statistics. Similarly, in consulting work with organizations, we have often seen barriers to communication and problem solving that at root are epistemologically based—

that is, based on conflicting assumptions about the nature of knowledge and truth.

The theory of experiential learning provides a perspective from which to approach these practical problems, suggesting a typology of different knowledge systems that results from the way the dialectic conflicts between adaptive models of concrete experience and abstract conceptualization and the modes of a active experimentation and reflective observation are characteristically resolved in different fields of inquiry. This approach draws on the work of Stephen Pepper, who proposes a system for describing the different viable forms of social knowledge. This system is based on what Pepper calls world hypotheses. World hypotheses correspond to metaphysical systems that define assumptions and rules for the development of refined knowledge from commonsense. Pepper maintains that all knowledge systems are refinements of common sense based on different assumptions about the nature of knowledge and truth. In this process of refinement he sees a basic dilemma. Although common sense is always applicable as a means of explaining an experience, it tends to be imprecise. Refined knowledge, on the other hand, is precise but limited in its application or generalizablity because it is based on assumptions or world hypotheses. Thus, common sense requires the criticism of refined knowledge, and refined knowledge requires the security of common sense, suggesting that all social knowledge requires an attitude of partial scepticism in its interpretation.

6 Understanding How Adults Learn

There can be few intellectual quests that, for educators and trainers of adults, assume so much significance and yet contain so little promise of successful completion as the search for a general theory of adult learning. Kidd has compared such a quest to the search for Eldorado, and reviews such as those of Dubin and Okun and Lasker and Moore confirm that individual learning behaviours are so idiosyncratic as to cast considerable doubt on any general assertions made about adults as learners. Learning activities and learning styles vary so much with physiology, culture, and personality that generalized statements about the nature of adult learning have very low predictive power. The most that Dubin and Okun will say in their review of eight school of learning theory is that different elements of the theories of these schools can help to explain certain limited phenomena. It is all the more surprising, therefore to hear confident generalizations regarding the characteristics of adult learning pour forth from the lips of graduate students and those presenting research papers.

According to Simpson, the two distinguishing characteristics of adult learning most frequently advanced by theorists are the adult's autonomy of direction in the act of learning and the use of personal experience as a learning resource. It is important to recognize, however, that self-direction in learning is not an empirically verifiable concomitant of adulthood. There are many individuals who are chronologically adult but who show a marked disinclination to behave in anything approaching a self-directed manner in many areas of their lives. Self-directedness is rather being advanced as a prescriptively defining characteristic of adulthood. Hence, for an act of learning to be characteristically adult, it will have to exhibit some aspect of self-directedness. But before examining further the nature and form of self-directedness, let us consider the range of theoretical perspectives that have been elaborated with regard to adult learning.

Principles of adult learning

To specify generic principles of learning is an activity full of intellectual pitfalls. Even if we leave aside the variables of physiology, personality, and cultural background, we still have to consider the implication of those developmental theories that hold that adults function in very different ways when responding to the societal and personal imperatives required of them in young adulthood, midlife, and old age. This suggests that the generic concept of adulthood is so broad and oversimplified as to be of limited use as a research construct.

Nonetheless, in the last twenty-five years a number of respected theorists have made an attempt to identify generalizable principles of adult learning in their quest to build a theory of adult learning that would aid practice.

The earliest of these attempts was that of Gibb, who presented the following principles of adult learning as the basis for a "functional" theory: Learning must be problem centered, learning must be experience centered, experience must be meaningful to the learner, the learner must be free to look at experience, goals must be set and pursued by the learner, and the learner must have feedback about progress toward goals. As with other specifications of principles of adult learning, however, what Gibb actually offers is a mix of pedagogic procedures and learning theory.

Following on from Gibb, Miller identified six crucial conditions for learning premised on the belief that at the higher levels of human development in adulthood cognitive models of learning, rather than behaviorist ones, were necessary. Thus, Miller argued that students must be adequately motivated to change behavior, they must be aware of the inadequacy of present behaviors, they must have a clear picture of the behavior required, they must have the opportunity to practice required behaviours, they must obtain reinforcement of correct behaviour, and they must have a sequence of appropriate materials. Despite Miller's emphasis on cognition, however, the conditions he specifies actually appear to fit the behaviorist paradigm.

In this review of theories of learning and their applicability to adulthood, Kidd identified the concepts that he felt informed the efforts of researchers into adult learning. These concepts were derived from the changing conditions of the adult's life-span, role changes required by changing societal imperatives, the egalitarian nature of adult student-teacher relationship, the greater differentiation of the organs and functions of adults, the self-directing nature of the adult, the physical, cultural, and emotional meaning of time, and attitudes surrounding aging and the prospect of death.

Gibb, Miller, and Kidd all based their arguments concerning the nature of adult learning on speculative grounds. Knox, however, produced a widely referenced study of adult development and learning in which he offered a number of broad observations concerning adult learning. In Knox's view, for example, adilts learn continually and informally as they adults to role changes and other adaptations. Adults' learning achievements are, however, thought to be modified by individual characteristics. The learning context of the physical, social, and personal characteristics sorrounding the learning act, as well as the content and pace of learning, also affect the learning achievement.

Knox also concludes that adults tend to underestimate their abilities and by over emphasizing school experience and interests, often perform below their capacity. Longitudinal studies show a retention of, and sometimes increases in learning abilities during adulthood, though cross-sectional studies tend to contradict this finding. Fluid intelligence decreases and crystallized intelligence increases in adulthood, and adults are able to learn as well in their forties and fifties as in their twenties and thirties, when and if they can control the pace of learning. Knox found the level of formal education to be associated much more with learning ability than with age, and recency of participation in formal education to be correlated with more effective learning. This finding, incidentally,was supported by earlier studies of Knox and Sjorgen and Knox, Grotelueschen, and Sjorgen.

Other findings from Knox's survey were that effective learning entailed an active search for meaning in which new tasks were somehow related to earlier activities. Knox found that short-term memory held stable until late adulthood and that long-term memory apparently improved with age. In terms of the mechanics of learning, practice was deemed to be initially important for the reinforcement of learning. Prior learning experiences had the potential to enhance or interfere with new learning. Older adults were able to learn most effectively when they set their own pace, when they took periodic breaks, and when learning episodes were distributed according to a rationale dictated by content. Knox found learning transfer to decrease with age, though his findings on problem-solving abilities were ambiguous, with a decline according to cross-sectional studies and a holding steady with longitudinal studies. The same difference was evident in studies undertaken of critical thinking. Task complexity and creativity were found to reflect individual differences and to be related only marginally to age. Knox concluded his summary in an optimistic vein, declaring that individual differences in learning were mostly unrelated to age and that "almost any adult can learn anything they want to, given time, persistence, and assistance."

One of the most ambitious attempts to identify the cardinal principles of adult learning and to put these to practical use is that of Brundage and Mackeracher. These writers identify thirty-six learning principles and draw from each principle facilitating and planning implications. For example, Brundage and Mackeracher believe that adults are able to learn throughout their lifetimes. Their past experience can be a help or hindrance to learning. It is through such experience, however, that individuals construct the meanings and value frameworks that in turn determine how they code new stimuli and information. Brundage and Mackeracher declare that past experience needs to be respected by teachers and that it can be directly applied to current situation for good educative effect. Those adults with positive self-concepts are thought to be more responsive to learning. Environments that reinforce the self-concepts of adults, that are supportive of change, and that value the status of learner will produce the greatest amount of learning. These writers judge adults to be strongly motivated to learn in areas relevant to their current developmental tasks, social roles, life crises, and transition periods. The development of skills requires adults to have a clear perception of desired behaviors. Reinterpreting past experience is time consuming and requires a redefinition of values and meanings.

In Brundage and the Mackeracher's view, voluntary participation in education and training is likely to create a nonthreatening climate of instruction that will result in a greater amount of learning. Learning will be further enhanced by regular feedback on progress, and positive feedback will act as a reinforcer for the pursuit of more learning. They think that a certain degree of arousal is necessary for learning to occur, whereas stress acts as a major block to learning. Brundage and Mackeracher also think adults learn best when they can control the pace of their learning and when they enjoy good health. However, because each individual will have an idiosyncratic learning style, it is dangerous to prescribe one mode of learning for all adults. Typical points of personally significant transition occur at the ages of twenty, forty, and sixty, and adults are said to be most responsive to learning programs that are related to these transition. Collaborative modes of teaching and learning will enhance the self-concepts of those involved and result in more meaningful and effective learning. A blend of learning for autonomous mastery of life with participation in groups is said to provide the greatest satisfaction for the learner.

As a result of a career-long exploration of the development of adults' learning-to-learn capacities, Smith has identified six general observation concerning the nature of learning: It is lifelong, it is personal, it involves change, it is partially a function of human development, it pertains to experience, and it is partially intuitive. Adult learners, however, also exhibit four essential characteristics. First, they have multiple roles and responsibilities, and this results in a different orientation to learning from that of children and adolescents. For example, they wish to make good educational use of the finite time they invest in education, they often take responsibility for identifying what they wish to learn, and they have a partially or fully formed self-concept Second, adults have accumulated many life experiences, and these result in distinct preferences for modes of learning and learning environments, such modes and environments comprising the essentials of individual learning styles. Third, adults pass through a number of developmental phases in the physical, psychological, and social spheres, and the transitions from one phase to another provide for the reinterpretation and rearrangement of past experience. Finally, Smith argues, adult experience anxiety and ambivalence in their orientation to learning. In particular, attempts to become more autonomous and self-directed are likely to involve threatening elements. Anxiety and stress may also be the result of job pressure, relational problems with significant others or of the adult's recalling the anxiety produced by earlier schooling experiences.

These four characteristics of adult learners-their special orientation to learning, their experiential base, their particular developmental changes and tasks, and their anxiety regarding learning generate, according to Smith, certain conditions for learning. Adults learn best when they feel the need to learn and when they have a sense of responsibility for what, why, and how they learn. Adults use experience as a resource in learning so the learning content and process must bear a perceived and meaningful relationship to past experience What is to be learned should be related to the individual's developmental changes and life tasks. The learning method used wil foster, to different degrees, the adult's exercise of autonomy. Adults will, however, generally learn best in an atmosphere that is nonhreatening and supportive of experimentation and in which different learning styles are recognized.

Darkenwald and Merriam present a list of eight principles of learning derived from learning process research that they believe can serve as guidelines for effective facilitation. They surmise that adults' readiness to learn depends on the amount of their previous learning, that intrinsic motivation produces more pervasive and permanent learning, that positive reinforcement is effective, that the material to be learned should be presented in some organized fashion, that learning is enhanced by repetition, that meaningful tasks and material are more fully and easily learned, that active participation in learning improves retention, and that environmental factors affect learning.

The specification of principles of adult learning undertaken by Gibb, Miller, Kidd, Knox, Brundage and Mackeracher, Smith, and Darkenwald and Merriam can be summarized as follows: Adults learn throughour their lives, with the negotiations of the transitional stages in the life-span being the immediate causes and motives for much of this learning. They exhibit diverse learning styles-strategies for coding information, cognitive procedures, mental sets and learn in different ways, at different times, for different purposes. As a rules, however, they like their learning activities to be problem centered and to be meaningful to their life situation, and they want the learning outcomes to have some immediacy of application. The past experiences of adults affect their current learning, sometimes serving as an enhancement, sometimes as a hindrance. Effective learning is also linked to the adult's subscription to a self-concept of himself or herself as a learner. Finally, adults exhibit a tendency toward self-directedness in their learning.

Such conclusions constitute a catechism familiar to educators and trainers of adults, as well as to learning theorists. They support Simpson's contention referred to at the outset of this chapter that adult learning theorists most commonly emphasize the experiential dimension of adult learning and stress the self-directedness of adults. Self-directedness is seen both as an empirically observable trait and as a propensity that should be encouraged. We should note, however, that the samples for the studies on which these generalizations concerning the nature of adult learning are based are culturally specific. To this extent, the research on adult learning is no different from that on its childhood equivalent, where, as a massive comparative study of primary school quality recently acknowledged, "With less than 5 per cent of the world's school population, the United States accounts for the majority of the world's empirical research on education".

In research into adult learning, moreover, the adults who form the sampling frames are for the most part ethnically homogeneous; that is, they are Causasian Americans. They are also drawn chiefly from middle-class or upwardly mobile working-class families, since this is the foremost clientele of continuing education programs. To base a comprehensive theory of adult learning on observations of white, middle-class Americans in continuing or extension education classes in the post-Second World War era is conceptually and empirically naive. It is, admittedly, cumbersome to preface every comment regarding adult learning theory with a caveat concerning the cultural and class specificity of one's sample and, hence, the limited generalizability of one's conclusions. Nonetheless, we fall far too frequently into the mistake of declaring that research reveals that adults, in a generic sense, learn in a certain way.

The eagerness to construct an empirically verifiable theory of adult learning is inextricably bound up with the quest for professional identity on the part of adult educators. As much as we would like to believe that the conduct and dissemination of research are motivated by an intellectually altruistic search for truth, it must be recognized that the definition of research "problems" and the selection of appropriate topics for investigation often reflect wider societal or professional imperatives. In this case, the reality is that the discovery of a set of learning behaviors that are unmistakably adult would be a cause for substantial professional celebration. If we could discover certain empirically verifiable differences in learning styles between children and adults then we could lay claim to a substantive area for research that would be unchallengeably the property of educators and trainers of adults. Such a claim would provide us with a professional identity. It would ease the sense of insecurity and defensiveness that frequently assails educators and trainers of adults in all settings when faced with the accusation that they are practicing a nondiscipline. The discovery of an empirically discrete domain of adult learning would grant to us an intellectual and professional raison d'etrae.

Such a revelation is unlikely to transpire for some considerable time, and it may be that the most empirically attestable claim that can be made on behalf of adult learning style concerns their range and diversity. Certainly we should be wary of claiming too high a level of generalizability for theories and concepts of adult learning derived from studies of white Americans in the lower-middle, amiddle and upper classes. How can we write confidently of adult learning style in any generic sense when we know little of the cognitive operations of, for example, Asian peasants, African tribespeople or Chinese cooperative labourers? Even within North American culture the empirical accuracy of generalizations about adult learning principles is highly questionanble in that we have few studies of the learning styles of Native Americans, while working-class adults, Hispanics, blacks, or orientals.

Applying new research instruments

The body of research literature discussed in the preceding section is one characterized by a mixture of speculation and empirically observed features of adult learning. The studies cited use a variety of methodological approaches and survey different samples, with the result that baseline comparisons are extremely hard to make. In recent years a number of researchers and practitioners have sought to synthesize the findings of this body of research into some framework of central adult learning principles. These central principles have then been converted into various research instruments that their designers believe can be applied to examining the extent to which principles of adult learning are being exemplified in any given practice setting. Two of these instruments the Principles of Adult Learning Scale (PALS) and the Andragogy in Practice Inventory (API)-were designed to test the presence of effective facilitation in practice rather than to provide empirical measures of forms of adult learning. In other words, both these instruments can be used to determine whether or not teachers or programmers are behaving as effective facilitators.

The PALS was devised by Conti to measure the extent to which practitioners supported the collaborative mode of teaching-learning that is usually cited by writers in the field as an exemplification of good practice. Conti surveyed a number of highly regarded theorists, including Freire, Lindeman, Houle, Knox, Kidd, Knowles, and Bergevin, to discover what they held to be the basic assumptions of adult learning. Not surprisingly, his findings are similar to those identified by the theorists revieed in the present chapter and to the central principles of effective facilitation. Hence, Conti found these writers to argue that "the curriculum should be learner centered, that learning episodes should capitalize on the learner's experience, that adults are self-directed, that the learner should participate in needs diagnosis, goals formation, and outcomes evaluation, that adults are problem centered, and that the teacher should serve as a facilitator rather than as a repository of facts".

For his doctoral dissertation, Conti determined "to develop and validate an instrument capable of measuring the degree to which adult education practitioners accept and adhere to the adult learning principles that are congruent with the collaborative teaching-learning mode". Drawing on Flanders's Interaction Analysis Categories that were established to assess student initiating actions, Conti constructed a five-point

Likert scale to record practitioner responses on a number of items that were based on collaborative principles but "reworded in behavioral terms compatible with realistic experiences of practitioners". For each of the items said to describe actions congruent with the collaborative mode, a separate item was included to describe mode. The PALS instrument was tested for construct, content, and criterion-related validity by two juries of adult education professors and fifty-seven practitioners in six separate programs. Testing for reliability was undertaken in phase two of the field testing by twice administering the scale to twenty-three adult basic education practitioners in chicago and comparing the congruence of the scores. The outcome of the study was a forty-four-item rating scale that Conti believes can be used to assess the effectiveness of collaborative modes in producing significant learning gains or to identify themes and topics around which in-service training activities could be designed for staff development.

Since its initial framing, Conti reports that the PALS has been used in numerous training workshops and that it has formed the basis for three research studies. Dinges used the instrument to study 265 Illinois ABE teachers in a staff development needs assessment, Pearson administered PALS to 99 midwestern training directors to investigate the relationship between managerial style and the adoption of collaborative modes of facilitation, and Douglass used it to examine the relationship of professional training in educating adults to the degree of support granted to the collaborative mode by 204 hospital educators and cooperative extension educators in the state of Washington. In addition, scores have been collected from 153 Texas practitioners in adult basic and allied health education. Not surprisingly, perhaps, the research of Pearson and kouglass indicates that the chief variable positively correlated with the adoption of a collaborative approach in management training, hospital education, and cooperative extension is the amount of previous formal education undertaken by these practitioners. It seems, from these studies at least, that those who are trained as educators of adults do indeed incorporate collaborative principles into their subsequent professional activities. After Conti's presentation of the PALS research at a recent conference of university adult educators in Britain, we can expect some cross-cultural validation of this instrument through comparative analyses of educators' use of the collaborative mode in Britain and North America.

Turning to the API, which was devised by Suanmali on the basis of Mezirow's interpretation of andragogy and his specification of a charter for andragogy, we find that it is a ten item inventory of educator practices. To help adults enhance their capability to function as self- directed learners, the education must:

1. progressively decrease the learner's dependency on the educators;

2. help the learner to understand how to use learning resources-especially the experiences of others, including the educator, and how to engage others in reciprocal learning relations;
3. assist the learner to define his/her learning needs—both in terms of immediate awareness and of understanding the cultural and psychological assumptions influencing his/her perceptions of needs;
4. assist learners to assume increasing responsibility for defining their learning objectives, planning their own learning programs and evaluating their progress;
5. organize what is to be learned in relationship to his/her current personal problems, concerns and levels of understanding;
6. foster learner decision-making-select learner-relevant learning experiences which require choosing, expand the learner's range of options, facilitate taking the perspectives of others who have alternative ways of understanding;
7. encourage the use of criteria for judging which are increasingly inclusive and differentiating in awareness, self-reflexive and integrative of experience;
8. facilitate problem-posing and problem-solving, including problems associated with the implementation of individual and collective action; rocognition of relationship between personal problems and public issues;

9. reinforce the self concept of the learner as a learner and doer by providing for progressive mastery; supportive climate with feedback to encourage provisional efforts to change and to take risks; avoidance of competitive judgment of performance; appropriate use of mutual support groups;
10. emphasize experiential, participative and projective instructional methods; appropriate use of modelling and learning contracts;

This instrument was examined by 147 members of the American Commission of Professors of Adult Education. The professors interviewed displayed a remarkable degree of agreement concerning the extent to which the practices identified above were indicative of good andragogical practice.

Finally, James and Manley have conducted small-scale Delphi investigations of what practitioners and professors of adult education regard as exemplary principles of practice that facilitate adult learning. Manley's review of the literature and her survey of eighteen members of the American Commission of Professors of Adult Education yield a familiar cluster of categories. The professors surveyed agree that adult learning is best facilitated when learners are engaged as participants in the design of learning, when they are encouraged to be self-directed, when the educator functions as a facilitator rather than didactic instructor, when individual learner needs and learning styles are taken into account, when a climate conducive to learning is established, when learners' past experiences are utilized in the classroom, and when learning activities are deemed to have some direct relevance or utility to the learners' circumstances.

In a more ambitious study, similar to Conti's researches, James devised the following set of basic principles of adult learning after a team of researchers had undertaken a search of articles, research reports, dissertations, and textbooks on adult learning.

1. Adults maintain the ability to learn.
2. Adults are a highly diversified group of individuals with widely differing preferences, needs, backgrounds, and skills.
3. Adults experience a gradual decline in physical/sensory capabilities.
4. Experience of the learner is a major resource in learning situations.
5. Self-concept moves from dependency to independency as individuals grow in responsibilities, experience and cconfidence.
6. Adults tend to be life-centered in their orientation to learning.
7. Adults are motivated to learn by a variety of factors.
8. Active learner participation in the learning process contributes to learning.
9. A comfortable supportive environment is a key to successful learning.

All nine principles were validated by a jury of national adult education leaders, and from these principles a questionnaire was constructed comprisig forty-five statements. The questionnaire was then administered to educators in five settings: hospital patient education, university extension programs, community colleges, business and industry, and agricultural extension. Some interesting differentials emerged in the study. Hospital patient educators, university extension instructors, community college instructors, and agricultural extension instructors all perceived themselves as implementing all the principles identified "frequently," while business and industry personnel perceived themselves as implementing principles one, two, and eight "sometimes" but the others "frequently." An interesting difference was also revealed regarding the principle ranked highest by these practitioners. In hospitals, universities, community colleges, and agricultural extension, principle nine "a comfortable, supportive environment is a key to successful learning"-was ranked as the most important. In business and industry, however, principle three "adults experience a gradual decline in physical/sensory capabilities"-was ranked highest. In contrast to the findings of Conti's PALS research, the principle referring most explicitly to collaborative modes of teaching and learning was ranked relatively low by instructors in all five settings. In particular, a number of studies of how practitioners do or do not conform to principles of good practice in real life program development settings will be examined. For the present it is enough to say that the foregoing instruments all represent contributions toward building a body of research on principles of good practice. The next chapter takes one particular aspect of the principles previously discussed-that of the adult's assumption of self-direction in learning-and examines the validity of this concept as an operational aim to be pursued in teaching-learning transactions. It also considers critically the research on which ideas about self-direction in adult learning are based, and it proposes a reinterpretation of this concept to take into account the extent to which self-directed adults exhibit an empowered autonomy in their learning activities.

7 The Role of the Adult Educator

The claims emerge from a perspective on practice which views adult education as an array of techniques focused largely upon the individual learner. Unhappily, the uncritical acceptance of an ideology of technique by many adult educators has tended to individuate the learner and reduce learning formats to narrowly defined lists of skills or 'competences'. The individuation of learners, via technicist programme design, overrides prospects for the acquisition competence through thoughtful discourse and reflective action with others. Relevant dimensions of social and community contexts in which the individual lives and works with others are thus overlooked in a technocratic pedagogical orientation.

This eventuality has been marked by a deployment of methodology on to the adult learning context under the banner of such artificially construed notions as self-directed learning, competency-based education, and learning how to learn. The heavy concentration of professionalized expertise and techniques on to the condition of the individualized adult learner evades a critical need for reflection about what adult educators themselves do and what they are. This points to deficiencies in modern adult education practice of both a practical and an ethical nature.

Some readers may be disturbed by an endeavour which undermines themes that have sustained the facade of more or less clearly defined and technicist modern practice of adult education. If this begins to crumble how do those of us who identify ourselves as belonging to a cadre of adult educators make sense of what it is we are and what it is we do in our occupational roles? This is where the notion of vocation comes in.

In an era when personal career advancement, professionalization, and upward social mobility are so much in vogue, the idea of vocation can seem oddly out of place—even pretentious. Yet this possibility is worth the risk, and can be avoided if the educational task confronting today's practitioners is not idealized. The term conveys a sense of thoughtful ethical commitment that some adult educators believe can be packaged and plugged into a modern practice just like any other component. This concern to add an ethical component, virtually as an after thought, is indicative of an occupation in search of an identity in which leading fugures who write the texts view practitioners as technicians rather than intellectuals.

In making vocation a paramount concern, we are not introducing a radically new orientation to the field of adult education but, rather, one that has been pushed to the margins by obsession with pedagogical technique and management by objectives. An ideology of technique, with it is commitment to technique and efficiency for the sake of technique and efficiency, leaves us with little appreciation of our past. It is, in effect, a historical. To an extent, then, we are evoking a sense of conviviality and shared responsibility exemplified in the notion of adult education as 'friends educating each other'. For the idealists among us and, one would hope, the idealist within each of us, this convivial dimension of adult education, sustained by generous aesthetic and moral impulses, is sufficient. However - and it is important to emphasize this for the benefit of those who fear that adult educators might become bogged down, irrelevantly, in some romanticized view of the world - such an orientation readily incorporates practical use of technique, technology, and concern for competent performance. In doing so, it leaves open prospects for on going discourse about whose interests ought to be served by such innovations, the underlying assumptions from which they emerge and the purposes to be achieved. A sense of vocation calls for a critical, self-reflective, practice of adult education.

A sense of vocation is not intended to imply some king of essence of adult education. Rather, it is invoked to underscore the significance of normative discourse about practice and 'passionate devotion' in the modern era when professionals, technicians, and bureaucrats tend to feel uncomfortable with such phraseology. In this regard, the quotation by Max Weber which opens this chapter is particularly instructive. Weber taught about what he pessimistically viewed as the inevitability of restrictive bureaucratizing effects which accompany modernity. And yet he managed to combine an ethical language of possibility with critical analysis and thought it important to talk in terms of vocational commitment.

Vocation refers to a calling and entails firm commitment to the performance of worthwhile activities that are not merely calculated to advance personal career aspirations or fulfil minimum fob expectations. It incorporates a strong ethical dimension, emphasizing an unavoidable necessity to make judgements about what should or should not be done and a readiness to take sides on significant issues. This pre-eminence of ethical considerations as a basis for day-to-day practice contrasits with the kind of pedagogical orientations and practices that are to be steered largely by technical rationality. Efficiency and expertise are secondary to the larger issues of human fulfilment and equality. They are not sufficient conditions for the development of a more just and humane society. Vocation streses personal responsibility on the part of the practitioner that cannot be abrogated by technicist prescriptions and preconceived formulations characterizing a cult of efficiency. It entails careful, self-conscious reflection about one's work- an intellectual commitment.

Clearly, the view of the practitioner's role taken here is different from that envisaged by much of the literature on the preparation of professional adult educators. It would be naive to suggest, for instance, that a revitalized emphasis on vocation has anything in common with a prevalent orientation that eschews careful critical reflection on the nature of practice and is largely concerned with distilling a narrow range of essential training skills from atheoretical psychologistic models. This incommensurability between the two viewpoints has not been understood by certain academics who now want to address the ethical concerns of a vocation, or critical practice, within the frame-work of a technical rationality. Their major preoccupation is not so much with examining the ends of adult education practice, unless effecting consensus is the end, as with the means. Vocational commitment, on the other hand, implies a refusal to be satisfied with the greater sophistication of technique, consensus-forming strategies, as the sole end of one's activity.

The fact that genuine vocational innterests cannot emanate from technical rationality does not, of course, preclude the intelligent use of technique by the reflective practitioner. In common usage, the term vocation is used in connection with a trade, occupation, or profession. It carries with it a clear-cut practical connotation along with an ethical component while avoiding a technical rationality which guides much of modern professionalized practice. Ethically based and practical orientations provide a context from which rational, non-coercive, decision-making about the relevant incorporation of technique can be carried out. The subordination of technique and technology to ethical and practical considerations is necessary for human-scale, less impersonal, programming and development of a king Ivan Illich has in mind when he writes about Tools for Conviviality.

The cult of efficiency in education has had a long run for its money, yet problems off illiteracy, human competence, and global survival are more starkly apparent than ever, fostered rather than alleviated by its myopic one-dimensional vision.

A need for continuing self-conscious reflection on what adult educators should do and should be cannot be sensibly dispensed with by the adoption of strategies emanating from the ideology of technique. Therefore, attention to ethical and practical matters intrinsic to the notion of vocation is necessary to make up for shortfalls in a modern practice of adult education wedded to pedagogical strategies derived from a pervasive technical rationality. The critique of technical rationnality and the disclosure of its many harmful effects on our everyday lives and future prospects for human survival on this planet is, in itself, an on-going mission for a committed critical practice of adult education.

The clear sense of mission that characterizes a concept of vocation could well be a source of uneasiness, especially among adult educators who harbour a secular humanist world view, since it is often associated with the imposition of religious ideas, accompanied by cultural invasion, by representatives of dominant national or ethnic interests. Critics of missionary endeavours are usually referring to inappropriate, intrusive strategies that have brought deleterious effects to the everyday lives of certain groups of indigenous people in ways not unlike those that emerged under the umbrella of technical rationalism. They point to evidence revealing that, in many parts of the world, the educational efforts of missionary undertakings have played a significant role, unwittingly or otherwise, in paving the way for economic exploitation and cultural imperialism. Adult educators need to be alert to this kind of pedagogical zeal and the ways in which it can support repressive initiatives. However, a missionary commitment does not have to entail irrational zealotry or unwarranted intrusion.

While it would be remiss of adult educators to loss over the potentially harmful once consequences of missionary endeavour, a sense of mission becomes integral to any extended educational process. It can scarcely be avoided where knowledgee in the formm of ideas, beliefs, strategies,, and know-how has been identified as beneficial and worthy of dissemination. Even teaching that it is usually best to attend to one's own affairs and personal development, leaving the learning of others to themselves, becomes a kind of missionary endeavour.' The idea of mission, then, despite the unfortunate connotations that often accompany it, should be sustained as a vital characteristic of any adult education endeavour. As a source of insight and inspiration, the notion of vocation is strengthened through its connection to a sense of mission.

In this regard, it is instructive to look, for example, in the work of Paulo Freire. A religious commitment can be clearly discerned in his pedagogy. In an essay entitled Paulo Freire: Educationalist of a Revolutionary Christian Movement, Peter Jarvis 'locates Freire within the prophetic tradition of the Christian Church' and examines the nature of his 'social and political involvement in the affairs of the day in order to influence the future'. Yet Freire's careful sense of educational mission, expressed through a pedagogy of the oppressed, is self-critical and extremely sensitive to the potentially harmful effects of intrusive strategies. Even if his approach is ultimately 'a utopian vision', as Jarvis suggests, Freire's pedagogy manifests itself in a thoughtful engagement with the concrete reality of people's everyday lives.

Fostering the notion of a reasonable sense of vission, with its clear-cut ethical connotations and reference to commitment, precludes the need for specialist writings on how to be ethical in adult education practice. Though such texts manifests an uncomfortable awareness that critical and moral issues are obscured by the technocratic bent of language which describes modern adult education practice, they are themselves cast in the same mould. For the most part, recent writings on ethics sustain the overall text of professional practice emanating from an ideology of technique. These texts on ethical conduct are plugged in as components of modern professionalized practice, but afer little prospect of creating an arena in which ethical discourse about everyday practice can flourish. They do not serve to unsettle the technicist paradigm, or averalll text, that characterizes contemporary adult education practice. Rather, they are systematically integrated into it so that existing frameworks for ensuring consensus and the predominantly non-reflective nature of discourse on practice remain intact.

A mission for adult education associated with a sense of vocation, rather than one embedded in an ideology of technique which promotes individualism, requires that ethical language is fostered as an integral aspect of adult education discourse. Thus, a value is placed on making judgements, and reflecting on their consequences, on an individual basis and in concert with others. This does presuppose a willingness to dissociate adult education practice from a paradigm,or an overall 'text', that seeks to define it in terms of technique.

The issue of competence

While a sense of mission and strong commitment is an essential constituent of vocation, it is not sufficient. Unless there is a deliberate effort to incorporate competent performance, the energy released through enthusiastic commitment and a sense of mission manifests itself in mere activism. The spontaneity and *ad hoc* strategies that characterize the latter may have short-term impressive effects. However, lacking the discipline and rational discourse that emanate from recognition of a need for competent and specific performance, activism fails to sustain any worthwhile line of endeavour over a significant period of time.

Competent performance as an aspect of vocation does not necessitate the mastery of predetermined number of skills, behaviours, or competences. It can be conceptualized in practical and ethical terms, without recourse to technical rationality of the kind. When attempts are made to define competent performance mechanically in terms of technocratic formulations and reductionistic competence statements, the thoughtful commitment that holds together the practical and ethical dimensions of vocational practice begins to unravel. Such formulations and mechanistic descriptions characterize competent performance in a way that forecloses on the need for us to reflect carefully on what it is we do, and what we are as adult educators.

By uncritically embracing technicist formulations and simplistic training models, adult education practice becomes prey to bureaucratic and political interests that seek to de-skill the adult educator's role. These interests are strengthened by a rationale that suggests fewer full-time educators are necessary or that their function—supported by pedagogical or adequately performed by part-timers. From this perspective, one of progressive de-skilling, talk of vocation and the necessity for thoughtful practical commitment becomes redundant. The implication is that anadequate formula to deal with any relevant activity can be readily accessed from a standardized package.

The problem of de-skilling that manifests itself in contemporary education and training practices has drawn sporadic critical commentary from a few writers. Yet such critique has been far from sufficient to spark resistance to a pervasive trend that, in North America especially, gains impetus from the competency based education movement. Under the banner of accountability, efficiency, effectiveness, and relevance, it promotes a narrow technicist approach to curriculum innovation that serves bureaucratic needs for external planning and decision-making but fails to provide relevant pedagogical support for practitioners who seek to enhance their own long-term competence as well as that of adult learners. In the present political climate, so-called competency-based education defines useful knowledge in the light of bureaucratic and corporate needs. Resistance to this destructive approach to education and training must accompany any serious attempts to recover a strong sense of vocation for the modern practice of adult education.

The rejection of predetermined technicist stipulations as a steering mechanism for assessing competent performance does not, of course, preclude appropriate use of technology as well as strategies for relevant action and legitimate knowledge from sources outside the immediate context. Technique and technology are not in themselves coercive. It is an irrational deployment of technique and technology for their own sake that becomes repressive.

A relevant approach to competent performance as integral to adult education as vocation requires a predisposition to take the pause necessary for identifying, focusing, and reflecting on the practical problem at hand. This process includes a recognition that the context in which it emerges will shape the problem at hand, to some extent or other, in a distinctive way. As one engages with the problem, it usually becomes apparent that well-proven recipes, techniques, and procedures can be applied. Where the problem presents itself in the form of a relatively familiar task - one that is largely of a technical nature, for example - it is typically accomplished without much in the way of self-conscious interpretative analysis. For most of us, competent performance at this level, through thoughtful practical experience, is often guided in the initial stages by someone who already has the required experience and competence.

Where the problem situation is more complex and other people are involved the interpretative aspect becomes more demanding. The practitioner should then take into account the motivations of other people involved in the context, the stakeholders, as well as his or her own motivations. An ethical dimension emerges; judgements have to be made and, subsequently, assessed. While familiar techniques can be relevantly incorporated, the situation at hand is likely to include some unfamiliar features that challenge the practitioner's powers of reflection and analysis. Evidence of competence is assessed from the way in which the familiar is deployed, with relevantly selected resources, to engage with unfamiliar dimensions at hand.

Loosely defined conjecturing and haphazrd activities do not constitute acceptable evidence of competent performance. The overall process needs to be systematic and calls for thoughtful, relevant structuring. We become better at it—more competent—with practice informed by careful reflection and analysis.

Careful reflection on our practice is not automatic. It is difficult, and not always feasible, to put aside a taken-for-granted stance as we go about our mainly routine day-to-day tasks. A disposition towards careful reflection, on our own account and in concert with others, has to be learned. We become more alert to its significance for improved practice with the recognition that reliance on prepackaged techniques alone will not suffice, and that reflection is required to identify the most appropriate strategies for the problem at hand. It should no longer still be necessary to refute the shaky assumptions underlying prepackaged formulations which purport to define expertly in pedestrian reductionistic terms the nature of competent performance for practitioners and learners.

Adult educators, along with other professionals, often suggest that competent performance is a matter of familiarizing oneself with theories and, then of putting these acquired theories into practice as relevant occasions arise. This does not seem to represent the case in any of the roles, professional or otherwise, we perform in our everyday world. 'Putting theory into practice', as the problem is often characterized, carries with it the presumption that a particular theoretical model can faithfully represent a particular order of reality. This deterministic notion, questioned even in the natural sciences, is not at all appropriate for the human sciences, which focus on the problem of human performance and provide much of the knowledge base for the helping professions. Though an understanding of theoretical constructions is important to any serious vocational endeavour, it is more efficacious to think in terms of engaging thought fully with theory and, then, putting ourselves into practice rather than putting theory into practice. In other words, serous engagement with theoretical models improves our potential as reflective practitioners, which in turn manifests itself in actual performance.

Efforts to identify clear-cut, comprehensive criteria for adult education practitioners vary from very detailed lists of the necessary competences for instructors, administrators, and counsellorrs to compilations of general commonsense advice about everyday practice. Examples of the latter are statements which advise practitioners to 'assess learning needs', develop effeective relationships with adult learners'., 'use relevant and effective instructional methods'. and so on. However, the notion that the qualities of an adult educator can be reduced to a determined number of measurable competences encompassing various levels of behaviour, knowledge, and attitudes is toublesome. It emerges directly from an ethos of thechnical rationality and inncorporates all the artificiality and shortcomings of a technicist orientation.

Vocational practice, incorporating careful reflection on its\ activities and aspiring to improved performance, will eschew the restrictive determinism of competency-based formats. These can only impair prospects for achieving and assessing competent performance from a basis of relevant reflection on practice in various adult education settings.

Rejection of a definitive list of competences, or set formulations, does not entail a careless approach to the achievement of high standards of performance. On the contrary, standards which support careful reflections on the requirements of the problem at hand can be set in each pedagogical context. The relevant dimensions of the task in hand will refer the thoughtful practitioner to appropriate standards. Dewey describes the process as follows:

> Thought runs ahead and foresees outcomes, and thereby avoids having to await the instruction of actual failure and disaster.

However, as the effectiveness, or otherwise, of the strategies employed is subsequently assessed, the question off whether or job appropriate standards have been met is directly addressed. As a matter of course the competent practitioner reflects on his or her own activity and its results.

Friends educating friends

The implication of all this is that adult education practice needs to be more concerned with the role of the educator, de-emphasizing a prevailing sharp and unremittting focus on the situation of the adult learner. A reorientation such as this will undoubtedly create unease, since it cuts across the grain formed by many authoritative texts on contemporary practice. The adult learner as a focus, or object, of professionalized strategies to render him or her self-directing has been at the core of adult education practice in recent years.

Deliberate initiatives emphasizing the paramount importance of careful reflection by adult educators on their own practice replaces a virtuallly obsessive preoccupation with learner-centred techniques. The learner, of course, should always matter in any pedagogical situation, but the kind of vocational commitment advanded here allows us to retrieve, in a rational way, the ethical notion of adult education as 'friends educating each other'. This describes a dialectical process where the teacher is also a learner and the learner, in learning, teaches the teacher. Thus the role of the practitioner becomes an even greater challenge. In remembering always to let the learner learn, the leader has to be open to being taught.

Although many adult educators would be readily inclined to acknowledge the notion of friends educating friends as a way to characterize their practice, very deliberate effort is required to retrieve its substantive ethical and democratic impulse. The categories which have emerged in recent times to define the adult learner together with their associated pedagogical techniques, create a distance between the learner and the adult educator, who becomes the expert. With the onset of professionally legitimized categorizations and techniques, caring for the adult learner in the convivial context of 'friends educating each other' is transformed into caring as an aspect of control. Terminology that rings of the corporate sector such as 'classroom management', 'contract negotiation', and 'human resource development' is deplyed to characterize the adult education endeavour. A critical task for vocation of adult education in contemprary society, then, is to uncouple itself from a tendency to transform an inclination for caring into a mechanism of control via an isolation of 'the adult learner' as an operational definition for catoeorization, and for the deployment of pedagogical technique.

A shift away from concentration on the adult learner as the target of categorization and transformation through technique to an emphasis on a clarification of the adult educator's role in the context of 'friends educating each other' opens out prospects for adult education as a vocation concerned with nurturing egalitarian values and commitments. In retrieving the idea of 'friends educating each other' as a prime characteristic of adult education practice, it is possible to sustain a concern for competence without distoring, through recourse to a technical rationality, the fragile dimension of a caring relationship.

A caring relationship within a pedagogical setting which is neither teacher nor learner centred does not mean that the educator should forgo responsibility by accepting in an uncritical way learners' opinions or views of what is relevant. An educational situation in which learners and teachers collaborate does not have to end up as a kind of buzz group where everything that is said goes unchallenged and is merely accepted as grist to the mill. The teacher remains responsible for organizing a pedagogical context where participants can collectively best fulfil their petential. where they all become subjects feglecting together on the process rather than the passive individualized objects of the process. Clearly the pedagogical situation envisaged here is altogether different from what H.C. Wilshire disdainfully refers to as 'the pecture sometimes drawn of teacher and students setting out in a condition of equal and happy ignorance to discover thins together'.

Theories of action perspectives

The perspective on adult education practice presented here is informed by theories of action. In contrast to pedagogical orientation, including those advanced under the rubrics of self-directed learning and learning how to learn, adult education that entails reflection on action is obliged to incorporate int its pedagogy a prime concern for social and institutionilized structures that inhibit a realization of genuine autonomous learning. While concern for motivations and for relevant aspects of learners' and teachers' personal history are of considerable significance to a theory of action approach, it eschews psychological categorization and a preoccupation with framing the educational context in terms of individualized deficiencies. The practitioner, then, is required to reflect upon and take into account the everyday social structures and institutionlized obstacles which get in the way of a natural inclination of people to learn in accordance with self-directed interests. The reified constructs of much of contemporary professionalized practice, such as self-directed learning and learning how to learn, do acknowledge the symptoms whereby many adults have internalized constraints that block self appropriated learning. Unhappily, they become part of the problem by legitimizing a focus on strategies that evade serious engagemnt with the root causes of these constraints embedded in our social structures. The evasion inherent in much of modern adult education practice is characterized by rhetoric on coping skills and competences, and by an insistence on the merits of diagnostic testing to identify individual deficiencies.

The purposeful incorporation into practice of critical thinking about how we and other adults act, and are acted upon, in our everyday social world is essential but not sufficient. We might all, eventually, become highly relativistic critical thinkers, identifying and debating about various assumptions and world views. Admittedly, this is an improvement on the taken-for-granted conscensus formation induced by naive faith in technique and the efficacy of coping skills. Unfortunately, it still leaves us with a need, overlooked by recent acvocates of critical thinking skills in education, to identify ourselves with the commitments and contexts from which we can make genuine democratically informed judgements for action in our everyday world. This is the kind of aspiration we found in the critical pedagogy of Paulo Freire, for example, until it was effectively sustained and overwhelmed in North America by the technical rationality guiding the overall text of modern adult education practice. As adult educators operating within this overall text, we can spark debate and 'trip the light fantastic' with talk about critical thinking skills and a nod or two in the direction of 'radical adult educators' without any of it making a tangible difference to our own practice.

Despite this prognosis, critical thinking guided by competence derived from relevant theory of action does hold out the prospect of adult education practice for social change. It is possible to envisage a pedagogical context, as we have learned from Habermas, where critical thinking makes problematic coercive and manipulative strategies, repressive manifestations of technical rationality, and the effective concealment of significant information. These are the conditions that can give critical thinking a genuinely transformative intent and allow for rational assessment of decisions emanating from critical discourse.

An understanding of significant theoretical analyses, such as those undertaken in the wide-ranging theory of communicative action which endeavours to provide reasons for genuinely democratic action, is integral to the role of a reflective practitioner. Serious commitment to adult education as vocation implies that its practitioners as intellectuals should be prepared to read and engage with theoretical texts as they begin to theorize their own practice. A vocational obligation to read thoughtful as well as how-to texts should not be undertaken with a facile expectation that increased practitioner effectiveness is to be achieved by merely putting early understood and readily explained theoretical constructs or models into practice. The vocational commitment for a reflective practitioner is more demanding. Theory requires pause for serious engagement if it is to enhance a reflective process through which the adult educator continues to develop his or her competence in practice.

The Theory of Communicative Action, for example, can provide us with further insights into the reasoning and commitments of Paulo Freire's emancipatory pedegogy. Habermas's outstanding theoretical analyses help substantiate Freire's commitment to dialogic interaction, his questioning of the banking concept of education that describes typical didactic endeavours to transfer bits of information from teacher to learner, and his notion of pedagogical praxis whereby reflection and action inter-twine and inform each other in a dialectical process. Most significantly, perhaps, is the fact that we can look to Habermas's theory of action to understand why emancipation should be at the core of adult education practice.

Many adult educators readily associate themselves with generous sentiments that seek to comit adult education practice to the cause of emancipation—freedom from oppressive and coercive structures—but, if they are committed to reflect on their practice, it is helpful to look beyond Freire to discover why this should be the case. Reference to the 'Theory of Communicative Action and, in particular, its account of the 'ideal speech situation' helps us in understanding why emancipation, freedom from coercive structures and systematic distortions, must be at the core of any adult education endeavour which aspires to a non-relativistic, genuinely democratic, endeavour for practice. It reveals, too, how dependence on the instrumentsl reasoning of a technical rationality distort the practical intent of any rational decision-making or learning process.

Although we have not even begun to explore the full potential of Jurgen Habermas's theoretical project as a primary source for reflection on adult education practice, the works of other important social theorists can assume importance in the development of reflective practice. It is not a matter of being familiar with all of them, a virtually impossible task for a full time academic, let alone a busy practitioner, or even of being thoroughly conversant with the entire theoretical programme of some. Nor should their works be envisaged as mutually exclusive, requiring that we pick and choose among them, like commodities on a supermarket shelf, to suit different occasions and contexts. Careful reading of selected works from social theorists, or good interpretors, who address the problems of rational decision-making and meaningful action reveals that they reinforce each other in developing our capacity to reflect critically upon practice and, hence, our competence as practitioners.

Even a very lengthy selection of social theorists whose work has relevance for adult education as vocation would be found wanting. However, it is reasonable, at this time, to count among other powerful theorists whose analyses merit serious attention as sources to enhance reflection on adult education practice. Alfred Schutz, Michel Foucault, Antonio Gramsci, Rosa Luxemburg, and John Rawls. Interest in the writings of these theorists has grown significantly during the past decade or so. Although representing somewhat different aras and cultural-linguistic backgrounds, their theoretical concerns overlap and have consequences for the way we need to think about adult education practice in today's society.

A further cautionary note is called for before a

brief account of the major theoretical concerns of these intelluctuals is offered. Some radical educators in recent years have drawn on the works of Habermas and Gramsci, as well as those of Freire and llich, treating them as blueprints for analysis and direct action within modern capitalist political economics. This kind of appropriation brings disillusionment. Accordingly there is risk that the works of these important thinkers will be shunted aside even from the margins of critical adult education practice rather than valued for the insights and inspiration to be derived from careful consideration of their theorizing and vocational commitment.

Alfred Schutz's phenomenological sociology, in particular his Theory of Relevance, describes the basis for an analysis of the problem of competent performance, revealing to us, at the same time, the artificiality and inadequacies of reductionistic approaches exemplified by pre-packaged competency based learning formats. In addition, we can look to Schutz's analysis of the structures and meanings of relevant actions in the everyday world, especially the concept of thematic relevance, to provide a theoretical justification for the problem posing orientation of Freire's pedagogy through which themes that have critical meaning in the everyday lives of adult learners are identified by them rather than being formulated for them. Schutz's publications, especially his collected papers, provide outstanding examples of how phenomenological investigations can give us insights into our experiences as learners and teachers, paving the way for significant new directions in adult learning and development theory.

The various ways power influences the nature, ownership, and dissemination of knowledge are a major concern of Michel Foucault's work. Engagement with his analysis of the interconnectedness of power and knowledge helps us understand how educational encounters are shaped by their incorporation into an overall system of control and surveillance. While this dimension of control and surveillance is more readily apparent in the education of particular groups of the adult population like prison inmates, the adult educator who reflects on her or his practice will begin to comprehend more vividly how it pervades most other formal education contexts. Foucault's analysis brings us face to face with coercive and manipulative structures which interfere with prospects for a pedagogy along the lines envisaged by Jurgen Habermas's Theory of Communicative Action. It can serve also to extend reflection on the kind of pedagogical concerns that emerge from Schutz's phenomenologically based theory of action. Not only should adult educators be concerned about the artificiality of learning formats that are reduced, in laundry list fashion, to a series of simplistic statements on skills, they also need to consider the extent to which these standardized formats lene themselves to the interests of management concerned as much with problems of control as with educational development. Efficient standardization that is the hallmark of reductionistic curriculum formats and of their potential to keep adult learners busy, if not very meaningfully busy, are a boon to education's bureaucrats, who place a high priority on centralization and control.

The research programme of Foucault, and of other theorists who address the problem of power and knowledge construction, obliges comitted adult educators to reflect upon whose interests are really being served by their practice. His notion of the specific intellectual, and the kind of active political commitment he intends it to convey, is very instructive for a vocation of adult education. Foucault questions the traditional view of intellectuals as authoritative spokesmen for universal themes such as truth and justice, and takes issue with a Marxian perspective in which 'the intellectual is thus taken as the clear individual figure of a universality whose obscure, collective form is embodied in the proletariat. Instead, a specific intellectual identifies the particular contexts and issues which are the locations for petentially effective resistance to coercive practices. With regard to prospects for social change, specific intellectuals do not presume to speak on behalf of the oppressed. Their proper role, when they share Foucault's critical perspective, is to reveal and challenge the actual institutionalized structures of oppression.

Antonio Grramsci's theoretical writings have rendered a comprehensive account of hegemony as a critical concept. It refers us to the prevailing state of affairs in which the predominant ideology, representing largely the interests of the most powerful groups within civil society and the economic-corporate sector, influences significantly the way most of us experience the world and conduct ourselves in most spheres of everyday life. The predominant ideology from this perspective is so pervasive that we internalize, in a taken for granted way, many of its imperatives on how we should experience the world. It tends to shape the very consciousness of our society. Particular significance attaches to the educational sphere where hegemonic interests can be advanced and sustained. The significance of ideological hegemony under both corporate capitalism and state capitalism has resided in its capacity to suppress, through one means of another, widespread awareness of its contradictions.

Gramsci's use of the concept of hegemony, however, does not leave us without the prospects for realizing social change through well thought out counter-hegemonic strategies. His writings identify education as a context for rational resistance to coercive aspects of prevailing hegemonic interests, for which it is a prime location. In positing also a notion of the 'organic intellectual', who identifies unequivocally the social groupings in whose interests he or she will be committed, Gramsci has left thoughtful adult educators with a vocational challenge and a keen sense of the contradictions inherent in everyday practice. His work poses starkly the kind of questions that can discomfort the reflective adult educator. Whose interests are we most effectively serving? Whose interests should we serve? Whose interests shall we serve?

As with Foucault, Gramsci's distinction between traditional intellectuals and those who recognize that they are not neutral and above the fray is significant for a vocation of adult education. It reminds us that adult educators, through their pedagogical meditation, have an intellectual role. Though he argued that 'every teacher is always a pupil and every pupil a teacher', Gramsci differs from Foucault in that he envisages organic intellectuals as leaders of popular education initiatives:

> A human mass does not 'distinguish' itself, does not become independent in its own right without, in the widest sense, organizing itself; and there is no organization without intellectuals, that is without organizers and leaders.

However, adult educators can, without inconsistency, draw on the work of both these outstanding intellectuals, since the 'human mass' identified by Gramsci is increasingly subject to the structures of surveillance and control that Foucault has so thooughly described.

The renowned Rosa Luxemburg—committed revolutionary, social theorist, and adult educator—was always clear-cut about whose interests she should serve. Luxemburg was very demanding of her working class adult students and demonstrated the kind of leadership and organizational proficiency that Gramsci, years later, attached to his notion of organic intellectualism. At the same time Luxemburg maintained that significant intellectualism. At the same time Luxemburg maintaine that significant social change towards genuine participatory democracy must emerge from spontaneously democraticaly motivated popular movements rather than from elite intellectual cadres acting on behalf of the people. Her classes in econoınics and history were conducted as dialectical discourse of a kind that is now pre-empted by individualizing pedagogical techniques. For luxemburg there was no need to talk in terms of teaching critical thinking skills. She believed that careful self-criticism was integral to self-education and that the development of their thinking processes was up to the students themselves.

Rosa Luxemburg was wedded to the idea that her task was to teach while learning. Thus, while immeasurably advancing her own competence, she avoided burdening herself with the limited perspective of the specialist. Two of her major works, Introduction to Economics and The Accumulation of Capital, came out of her teaching activities. Above all, though, Luxemburg's vocational commitment exemplifies caring for others, consistentency, and immense personal courage.

Besides teaching adult education classes, Luxemburg's pedagogical mission was te writing of birlliant polemics which have their grounding in her important theoretical work.

An reflection on the role of adult education as

vocation would be enriched by the arguments advanced by John Rawls in A Theory of Human Justice. Though seemingly less radical than Gramsci or Luxemburg, his work marks a significant endeavour to describe a notion of justice that does not leave the individual subservient to a technical rationality serving institutionalized legal and economic interests. At the core of his thory is the principle that no individual should be a means to the ends of predominant societal interests. A just society seeks to maximize, through ethical and practical means, the advantage of its least advantaged members. Thus, although its concern is with individual agency rather than with the prospects of collective experience, Rawls's work is distinctly humanistic.

Rawls is more readable, perhaps deceptively so, than most theorists and his prose is relatively free of the kind of phraseology that may make the writings of Habermas, Foucault, Gramsci, and Luxemburg appear too politically laden for many American adult educators in particular. It is worth emphasizing at this juncture, though, that the analyses of these theorists, and others who write in similar vein, constitute a comprehensive critique of the effects of a technical rationality and its attendant mechanism of control that prevail in both the corporate, 'free enterprise'. capitalistic economies of the West and the state capitalism that has steered 'Soviet economies'.

Many readable and thoughtful interpretations of important social theoretical writings that can inform our reflections on practice are now accessible. The significance of both original writings and subsequent careful interpretations lies in their potential for helping to heighten the level of critical discourse about adult education practice, not in any tidy solutions we may hope to glean from them. By the same token, thoughtful practitioners will not be inclined to take the theorists on faith. The contribution of social theories of action to an on-going conversation about adult education as vocation is enhanced by subjecting their assumptions and findings to critical assessment. Ultimately, however, the nature and quality of practice emerging from a vocation of adult education depend upon our own capacity to reflect critically upom what we are and what we do as adult educators.

Making music together

Theory of action perspectives, then, are helpful to reflection on the kind of practice which exemplifies a sense of vocation. They point us to prospects for the realiozation of a more self-assured adult education practice while retrieving its ethical, convivial, vision of 'friends educating one another': one in which 'every teacher is always a pupil and every pupil a teacher'. This renewed prospect for ethical, rationally conceived, adult education practice as vocation is juxtaposed against pedagogical strategies derived from an ideology of technique that focuses on correcting learner deficiencies rather than upon prevailing institutionalized structures that get in the way of self-induced learning and which create many of the learning disabilities in contemporary society.

In breaking away from the parametres of the prevalent overall 'text' which more or less describes the arena for contemporary adult education practice, it is not necessary to start from scratch. There are many adult education intiatives that already exemplify, through the nature of their commitment, the kind of orientation outlined for adult education as vocation. Among adult educators who work in difficult institutional circumstances, these are those who already conceptualize their roles along lines described here, confronting day-to-day contradictions in thoughtful, realistic, terms. Their pedagogical situations provide useful examples of what is needed to realize a committed, reflective practice of adult education in contemporary society and should be affirmed as legitimate contexts from which to draw analysis and inspitation. The notion of 'friends educating one another' forged in such contexts refers us to I-thou relationships where a sense of personal responsibility for others renders redundant bureaucratic demands for mechanistic, distancing, accountability measures. So we are not at all envisaging a casual, haphazard, pedagogical process. Freire's pedagogy fosters I-thou relationships, but recognizes that the educator has a duty to work on creating egalitarian situations:

> At the point of encounter there are neither utter ignoramuses nor perfect sages; there are only men who are attempting, together, to learn more than now know.

This does not call for self effacement where

teacher competence and leadership qualities are deliberately down-played at the expense of overall performance. The adult educator's performance, in this regard, can be likened to that of the jazz virtuoso who creates situations which enable the other band members to extend their own capacities. Making music together provides an apt metaphor for the kind of pedagogical practices that constitute a vocation of adult education. For Alfred Schutz the musical experience invokes 'the mutual turning-in relationship upon which alone all communication is founded'. Through this kind of relationship 'the' "I" and "Thou" are experienced by both participants as a "we" in vivid presence'. Myles Horton, founder of the internationally renowned Highlander Folk School, would agree, though, no doubt, in more down-to-earth terms. For over half a century making music together has been a vital feature in Highlander Folk School's continuing endeavour, through adult education, to realize a more just social order:

> Music plays a critically important part in this process. Seldom do people gather at Highlander without someone around to make music. People learn about unity by acting in unison. Theey learn about democracy by acting democratically.

And the 'synthesis of person, group, time, place, purpose, and problem that characterizes collective learning at Highlander has required a very high order of vocational commitment. As with Paulo Freire and Richard Tawney, it is possible to locate Horton's sense of commitment to adult education as a vocation for the realization of a more just society within the Christian tradition.

The intent is to examine prospects for unravelling the constraints of the predominant perspective that largely commits modern adult education practice to an ideology of technique, we are still mindful that actual practice on a day-to-day basis has to deal with the way things are, not with what we would wish them to be.

8 Adult Life-world Concerns and Protection of the Commons

The Constituents of the life-world which manifest themselves in the way human beings relate to each other, and to the natural environment. Habermas, for example, talks about the destruction of these life-world constituents, and hence the disintegration of locations which they sustain, in terms of 'realms of experience and forms of life that are threatened with being eroded, undermined, and washed away by the dynamics of economic growth and bureaucratization'. Examples of this tendency, characterized by Ivan Illich as 'erosion of the commons', have been addressed in previous chapters where prospects of engaging woth the attendant problems in the context of contemporary adult education were raised.

Mostly, the adult's life-world is mace up of routine day-to-day activities that are accomplished, effectively of otherwise, in a taken-for-granted manner. Although we expect to encounter difficulties from time to time, even the occasional serious set-back, these activities usually take place within a reasonably familiar and well-defined context. Therefore, in a commonsensical way, we are inclined to take them for granted rather than posing them as problematic. This essentially pragmatic mental stance that accompanies our everyday adult activities is described by Alfred Schutz as the natural attitude in which we suspend all scepticism during the pursuit of our daily affairs about the immediate events, environmental effects, and societal contexts in which we are involved. Unfortunately, this necessary pragmatic stance of the natural attitude leaves us increasingly vulnerable to the harmful consequences of decisions steered predominantly by technical rationality and of ill-conceived technological innovation. It becomes more and more an imperative for adults to acquire the capacity to put aside the natural attitude of their everyday life-world and adopt a sceptical approach towards taken-for-granted innovations 'necessary for progress', supposedly {acceptable' impositions as the price of progress, and seemingly authoritative sources of information that describe for us the landscapes of contemporary social reality. Clearly, if the concerns of this book are taken seriously, a critical capacity of this kind cannot be engendered on a wide scale by the deployment of courses on critical thinking skills and essays on how to think critically. Such instrumentalization of the problem, in a taken-for-granted manner, defeats its purpose. A capacity to replace the mental stance of the natural attitude in relevant situations that are presently taken for granted requires an unrelenting pedagogical effort. Only through a commitment to embracing a continuing critical reflection on practice and a determination to incorporate critical though (not merely debating pros and cons) within all education settings can adult educators help counter the debilitating consequences to our life-world of an ideology of technique reinforced by its taken-for-granted acceptance.

This issue of professionalization explored in previous chapters shows the way technical rationality supports a widely taken-for-granted dependence on experts, leading to a replacement of practical activities that formerly belonged to the everyday life-world of reasonably competent, attentive adults. Through legalistic means, professionalization has resulted in the transference to experts of many vital activities that were, and can still be, adequately performed within the domain of the everyday life-world. The analysis of Jürgen Habermas is again instructive in this regard:

> The bureaucratization and legal regulation of private and informal spheres of action: and above all the political-administrative incorporation of school, family, education, and cultural reproduction in general-these developments make us aware of a new problem zone that has arisen on the borders separating system and life-world.

Rather than questioning and offering informed resistance to a trend that has led to a significant de-skilling within life-world contexts, the modern practice of adult education has lent its weight to the world of the specialists the system-world.

To the simplistically offered objection that one would not go to a non-specialist for surgery, antibiotics, or advice on litigation, there is an obvious response that the retrieval and development of competence in personal care home economics, and community based services would considerably, reduce dependence on surgeons, pharmaists, lawyers, and other specialists.

Apart from engendering critical discourse among professionals about professionalization and identifying problems induced through an unexamined technical rationality that undermines vital aspects of our everyday life-world adult educators can light upon locations and concerns where a thoughtful pedagogy would help sustain life-world interests. Neighbourhood issues, the relationship between adults and children, concerns about health, ecology, concerns about military installation - these are all cooled out by the taken-for-granted encroachment of a technical rationality that can still be made problematic through an informed, critical pedagogy. Nor need pedagogical involvement with these concerns be confined to informal community-based contexts. Schools, colleges, prisons, the work-places-most formal institutional settings, in fact - are locations where practical critique can be undertaken through a pedagogy favouring the enhancement of communicative competence over educational strategies merely intended to alleviate concerns of the non-experts. Clearly, there are difficulties in practising such a pedagogy within the very institutions from which threats to life-world values emanate, but the stresses and crises of modern institution always provide opportunities for alternative kinds discoursse where management does not shortsightedly favour a degree of authoritarianism that becomes dysfunctional to its own interests. It is important for adult educators to foster alternative discourses within large scale institutionalized settings because the preservation of what is vital in our everyday life-world depends upon the fostering of its vital, communicative, constituents within the system-world. The task is to humanize the latter so that it enhances rather that depletes the former. Adult educators, then, have a significant role to play in taking a piece of the 'commons', so graphically described by Ivan Illich, into contemporary society's industrialized, commercialized, and bureaucratized organizations, although Illich himself would maintain that we should look exclusively to alternative community-based arrangements for the preservation of traditional values. Despite the relevance for us of Illich's notions of the 'commons' and 'vernacular values', a hardier, less romanticized, pedagogy in line with the theoretical and practical commitments of Gramsci and Hsbermas holds out more promise of social transformation, since it extends to the institutions of the system-world from which we cannot entirely escape. Unlike Illich these two theorists and activists recognize that industrial and bureaucratic organizations, though steered by an ideology of technique, provide significant locations for retrieving genuinely democratic communicative value.

At the same time, the predicament of the family in contemporary society presents a challenge for adult education to create learning situations, transcending class, socio-economic and ethnic boundaries, that explore how men and women can live together and, more importantly, raise children in caring relationships. The typical family unit headed by a patriarchal male as sole bread-winner becomes increasingly less typical while it is idealized by state interests wich undermine traditional family autonomy through reformist interventions. Even those middle-class families which seems to approach the ideal are subject to external influences and intrusions that serve to erode traditional patriarchal and domestic functions, add to the emotional turmoil of growing children, and bring further ambiguity to the roles of wife and mother. Clearly, the retention of an idealized typical family unit from which all other domestic arrangements for living together are defined is now extremely problematic. A concerned pedagogy can scarcely escape from the critical everyday life-world considerations touched upon here. They are situated within what Habermass describes as 'the new problem zone'. Much more research is required to reveal the full extent of problems that suggest a diminishing ability to inculcate future generations into a community ethic and value-oriented action that will sustain it. Adult education has a role to play in examining, and offering, options to nihilistic tendencies that cannot now be fully countered by the disappearing traditional family unit. A useful start in a hopeful direction could be made by incorporating a critical dimension to, and completely re-conceptualizing, the subject that takes the family and domestic arrangements as its focus-home economics.

Government and corporate interests are now having to confront increasing alarm about the destruction of valuable environmental non-renewable resources. The extent of the crisis presses for relevant involvement of adult educators within the environmental movement which is gaining momentum on a global scale as governmental and corporate efforts to alleviate public concerns without dealing with their vilidity are being systematically challenged. Apart from bringing their organizational capacities to bear through direct participation in the movement and through dissemination of information to critically engage complacent, but methodically presented, corporate public relations reports, adult educators have a significant role to play in introducing ecological themes into regular educational programming and cladssroom teaching. Similar opportunities exist for the development of a more thoughtful pedagogical involvement with anti-nuclear and peace movements, with alternative community-based, non profit, initiatives such as food co-ops, credit unions, co-operative housing and alternative technology, and with movements committed to the preservation of cultural, linguistic, and regional identities. These alternative spheres of resistance to both corporate and state capitalism make problematic areas of concern that are otherwise overlooked by an overly technocratic orientation to progress. In view of their healthy practical concern for the well-being of the species and the survival of our planet over capitalistic or state-determined politico-economic imperatives, these spheres of resistance are eminently progressive. It is to be hoped that in subsequent phases of their development, and this is where adult education can surely help, they will place more emphasis on transforming bureaucratized and governmental structures into a means for supporting and enhancing precious dimensions of the life-world exemplified by genuinely democratic interactions. People create the structures of the system-world; people can bring them in hand.

Adult educators in many parts of the world already incorporate the kind of commitments outlined above into our pedagogical practice. The International Council for Adult Education, in particular, publishes accounts of initiatives consistent with a transformative pedagogy sensitive to adult life-world concerns and the protection of the commons. Insights and imaginative contemporary strategies directly relevant to a transformative practice of adult education can be derived from essays on community development initiatives, of then'grass-roots' genre rather tha 'top-down' approaches, and from the activities of popular movements which are not yet overly attentive to all the significant dimensions of their adult educational function. There is, then, a discernible and active arena in which careful work is undertaken on behalf of collective and public concerns rather than those of corporate and individualistic interests, and where transformative pedagogy already manifests itself. No adult educator needs to be talking about transformative practice of critical theory in isolation from some relevant location where the discourse can be put to the test.

An optimistic perspective, supported by an enlightened pedagogy envisages the life-world and system-world acting upon each other to mutual benefit. Initiatives to protect life-world interests can add greater democratic communicative capacity to the system-world of corporate and bureaucratic decision-making, which thus becomes more readily inclined to act rationally in conserving the 'commons' of Illich's metaphor. But the educational effort is necessary. There are still may influential people who find no problem at all with the notion of constructing mines and corporate enterprises in wilderness parks which, in effect have already been legally designated as 'commons'. Some may even resort to violence in asserting a right to savage the 'commons'. While this chapter was being written, the Manchester Guardian Weekly reported that Francisco Mendes, internationlly known defender of the Amazon rain forests and aboriginal rights, had been murdered. The man who surrendered himself to the police is said to have been a rancher opposed to the struggle to the rain forest. Francisco Mendes, among others, has established how wasteful and destructive ranching is of rain forest resources and the extent of involvement in forest devastation on the part of large corporations such as Xerox, Georgia Pacific, the Dutch company Bruynzeel and the Japanese Toyomenka. As a result of his educational activities, the World Bank and the Inter-American Regional Bank were persuaded in 1988 to withhold financing from the region 'until serious environmental protection measures had been taken'. But the stakes are high.

Implicit in the alternative orientations described in the previous section is a strong affinity with moves towards decentralization and against further centralization. It is in this regard that adult education can well afford to examine its own practice, where prevailing trends to centralize the curriculam in line with a management perspective calls for continuing scepticism. In addition to advancing critiques concerning ethical and practical claims which accompany the deployment of centralized curriculum disigns, adult educators should make every reasonable effort to be meaningfully involved in curriculum initiatives. Meaningful involvement would require resistance to suggestions that a mere endorsement of already determined criteria and frameworks is sufficient. Failure to realize meaningful participation does not necessarily incapacitate adult educators working in formal institutional settings, but a disinclination to struggle for such involvement and to question top-down centralizing initiatives scarcely qualifies them to talk about teaching critical thinking to their students.

While the trend towards centralized administration and design of the adult education curriculum has encountered critical assessment, other centralizing measures within adult education agencies seem to have been accepted in a taken for granted manner. Sometimes, they are readily embraced by those who ought to be asking the questions. In any event, if the widely espoused notion of 'empowering adult learners' through the teaching of critical thinking is to be taken seriously, adult educators must attend to the way that top-down initiatives within their own organizations effectively curtail prospects for genuine dimocratic discourse and for the relevant participation in decision-making that this implies. A careful analysis of the context and the motivations from which these initiatives emerge usually reveals some possibility of less formalized appropriate communicative discourse that sustains countervailing strategies. The latter, viewed individually and in the short run, may not seem immediately significant, but they do shape the course of events even in quite authoritarian institutions where adult educators work such as prisons, the military, hospitals, and public schools. Alternative strategies that do arise as part of an informal communicative structure cannot be totallly eliminated or completely steered through a heavily centralized administrative format unless the right to question and resist, even in subtle forms, is surrendered.

Some initiatives towards centralization and management of resources do, of course, make sense. This is the case with distance education programmes created to meet the needs of people who do not have ready access to format learning opportunities in line with their educational needs. Here too, through, careful involvement is required of the part of committed adult educators to ensure that enthusiasm for the available technology and a capability to neatly pre-package learning materials at central locations do not supersede the need for locally oriented educational support. Without the latter, which usually means provision for some face-to-face interaction between educator and students, distance education can become a vehicle for a kind of cultural invasion in which communities are envisaged as 'reception sites' for the technology and methodological approaches of distance education specialists. This is most evident, for example, where distance education courses emanate from a central location within the dominant culture for delivery to aboriginal people in remote areas. More critical analysis is needed to assess the homogenizing effects of distance education and its potential as a delivery system to serve governmental and large scale corporate interests rather than those of people in their community settings. In the meantime, adult educators should be on guard to ensure that distance education is not shaped largely by technocrats and those with those with a bent for implementing overarching curriculum design.

Issue has to be taken with those who claim that the price of genuine participatory democracy in our institutional arrangements is continuing inefficiency. This book is not a plea for the relegation of a concern for efficiency, for the complete abandonment of technical rationality, or for a bizarre, romanticized stance against technological development of any kind. A technical rationality, tempered by careful consideration, practical, ethical, and aesthetic in line with Habermas's notion of a superior rationality embedded in genuinely democratic communicative action, is conducive to the sustenance of vital life-world interactions and to the protection of the 'commons'. As an integral aspect of a more wholesome communicative action, is conducive to the sustenance of vital life-world interactions and to the communicative rationality, which it seeks to support rather that determine, technical rationality becomes most relevant in the development of more benign technologies that serve, first and foremost, democratically conceived community needs rather than those determined predominantly by state and corporate interests. Contemporary adult education practice can play a significant role in helping the realization of this prospect, but a determined effort is required to break with the ideology of technique which shapes its present course. The question is whether adult educators are prepared to master the insight, imagination, and commitment needed for the kind of critique of their own practice implied in this quotation:

There are increasing numbers of concerned persons today who seek to mitigate the fissiparous, socially fragmenting effects of technical reason by calling for a renewed devotion to 'common social values'. But the calls for common social values are almost never accompanied with the demand for a critical questioning of the dominance of technical reason in modern society as the only recognized source of knowledge.

Such a demand can elicit an authentic pedagogical response only from a vocation of adult education that is committed more to the life-world concerns described in this chapter than to a self absorbed preoccupation with professionalization and to the deployment of technocratic curricula based on an individualizing 'adult learner characteristics' rationale.

9 The Interpersonal Relationship in the Facilitation of Learning

We wish to begin this chapter with a statement that may seem surprising to some and perhaps offensive to others. It is simply this: 'Teaching, in our estimation, is a vastly over-rated function."

Having mads such a statement, we scurry to the dictionary to see if we really mean what we say. Teaching means 'to instruct'. Personally, we are not much interested in instructing another in what she should know or think, though others seem to love to do this. 'To impart knowledge or skill'. Our reaction is, why not be more efficient, using a book or programmed learning? 'To make to know'. Here my hackles rise. We have no wish to make anyone know something. 'To show, guide, direct'. As we see it, too many people have been shown, guided, directed. So we come to the conclusion that we do mean what we said. 'Teaching is a relatively unimportant and vastly overvalued activity.

But there is more in my attitude than this. We have a negative reaction to teaching. Why? we think it is because it raises all the wrong questions. As soon as we focus on teaching, the question arises, what shall we teach? What, from our superior vantage point, does the other person need to know? We wonder if, in this modern world, we are justified in the presumption that we are wise about the future and the young are foolish. Are we really sure as to what they should know? Then there is the ridiculous question of coverage. What shall the course cover? This notion of coverage is based on the assumption that what is taught is what is learned; what is presented is what is assimilated. We know of no assumption so obviously unttue. One does not need research fo provide evidence that this is false. One needs only to talk with a few students.

But we ask ourself, 'Are we so prejudiced against teaching that we find no situation in which it is worthwhile?' we immediately think of my experiences in Australia long ago. Becamed much interested in the Australian Aborigines. Here is a group that for more than 20,000 years has managed to live and exist in a desolate environment in which modern man would perish within a few days. The secret of the Aboriginal's survival has been teaching. He has passed on to the young every shred of knowledge about how to find water, about how to track game, about how to kill the kangaroo, about how to find his way through the trackless desert. Such knowledge is conveyed to the young as being the way to behave, and any innovation is frowned upon. It is clear that teaching has provided him the way to survive in a hostile and relatively unchanging environment.

Now I am closer to the nub of the question that excites me. Teaching and the imparting of knowledge makes sense in an unchanging environment. This is why it has been an unquestioned function for centuries. But if there is one truth about modern man, it is that he lives in an environment that is continually changing. The one thing I can be sure of is that the physics that is taught to the present-day student will be outdated in a decade. The teaching in psychology will certainly bo out of date in twenty years. The so-called 'facts of history' depend very largely upon the current mood and temper of the culture. Chemistry, biology, genetics, and sociology are in such flux that a firm statement made today will almost certainly be modified by the time the student gets around to using the knowledge.

We are, in my view, faced with an entirely new situation in education where the goal of education, if we are to survive, is the facilitation of change and learning. The only man who is educated is the man who has learned how to learn; the man who has learned how to adapt and change; the man who has realized that no knowledge is secure, that only the process of seeking knowledge gives a basis for security. Changingness, a reliance on process rather than upon static knowledge, is the only thing that makes any sense as a goal for education in the modern world.

So now with some relief I turn to an activity, a purpose, which really warms me—the facilitation of learning. When I have been able to transform a group—and here I mean all the members of a group, myself almost beyond belief. To free curiosity; to permit individuals to go charging off in new directions dictated by their own interests; to unleash the sense of inquiry; to open everything to questioning and exploration; to recognize that everything is in process of change - here is an experience I can never forget. I cannot always achieve it in groups with which I am associated, but when it is partially or largely achieved, then it becomes a never-to-be forgotten group experience. Out of such a context arise true students, real learners, creative scientists and scholars, and practitioners, the kind of individuals who can live in a delicate but ever-changing balance between what is presently known and the flowing, moving, altering problems and facts of the future.

But do we know how to achieve this new goal in education or is it a will-o'-the wisp that sometimes occurs, sometimes fails to occur, and thus ofers little real hope? My answer is that we possess a very considerable knowledge of the conditions that encourage self-initiated, significant, experiential, 'gut-level' learning by the whole person. We do not frequently see these conditions put into effect because they mean a real revolution in our approach to education and revolutions are not for the timid. But we do find examples of this revolution in action.

We know—and I will briefly mention some of the evidence—that the initiation of such learning rests not upon the teaching skills of the leader, not upon scholarly knowledge of the field, not upon curricular planning not upon use of audiovisual aids, not upon the programmed learning used, not upon lectures and presentations, not upon an abundance of books, though each of these might at one time or another be utilized as an improtant resource. No, the facilitation of significant learning rests upon certain attudinal qualities that exist in the personal relationship between the facilitator and and the learner.

We came upon such findings first in the field of psychotherapy, but now there is evidence that shows these findings apply in the classroom as well. We find it easier to think that the intensive relationship between therapist and client might possess these qualities, but we are also finding that they may exist in the countless interpersonal interactions between the teacher and pupils.

Qualities that facilitate learning

What are these qualities, these attitudes, that facilitate learning? Let me describe them very briefly, drawing illustrations from the teaching field.

Realness in the facilitator of learning

Perhaps the most basic of the essential attitudes is realness or genuineness. When the facilitator is a real person, being what she is entering into a relationship with the learner without presenting a front or a facade, she is much more likely to be effective. This means that the feelings that she is experiencing are available to her, available to her awareness, that she is able to live these feelings, be them, and able to communicate them if appropriate. It means that she comes into a direct personal encounter with the learner, meeting her on a person-to-person basis. It means that she is being herself, not denying herself.

Seen from this point of view it is suggested that the teacher can be a real person in her relationship with her students. She can be enthusiastic, can be bored, can be interested in students, can be angry, can be sensitive and sympathetic. Because she accepts these feelings as her own, she has no need to impose them on her students. She can like or dislike a student product without implying that it is objectively good or bad or that the student is good or bad. She is simply expressing a feeling for the product, a feeling that exists within herself. Thus, she is a person to her students, not a faceless embodiment of curricular requirement nor a sterile tube through which knowledge is passed from one generation to the next.

It is obvious that this attitudinal set, found to be effective in psycho-therapy, is sharply in contrast with the tendency of most teachers to show themselves to their pupils simply as roles. It is quite customary for teachers rather consciously to put on the mask, the role, the facade of being a teacher and to wear this facade all day, removing it only when they have left the school at night.

But not all teachers are like this. Takd Barbara Shiel She gave her pupils a great deal of responsible freedom, and I will mention some of the reactions of her students later. But here is an example of the way she shared herself with her pupils—not just sharing feelings of sweetness and light, but anger and frustration. She had made art materials freely available, and students often used these in creative ways, but the room frequently looked like a picture of chaos. Here is her report of her feelings and what she did with them.

I find it maddening to live with the mess—with a capital M! No one seems to care except me. Finally, one day I told the children... that I am a neat orderly person by nature and that the mess was driving me to distraction. Did they have a solution? It was suggested there were some volunteers who could clean up... I said it didn't seem fair to me to have the same people clean up all the time for others - but it would solve it for me. 'Well, some people like to clean,' they replied. So that's the way it is.

I hope this example puts some lively meaning into the phrases I used earlier, that the facilitator 'is able to live these feelings, be them, and able to communicate them if appropriate'. I have chosen an example of negative feelings because I think it is more difficult for most of us to visualize what this would mean. In this instance, Miss Shiel is taking the risk of being transparent in her angry frustrations about the mess. And what happens? The same thing that, in my experience, nearly always happens. These young people accept and respect her feelings, take them into account, and work out a novel solution that none of us, I believe, would have suggested. Miss Shiel wisely comments, 'I used to get upset and feel guilty when I became angry. I finally realized the children could accept my feelings too. And it is important for them to know when they've "pushed me". I have my limits, too.'

Just to show that positive feelings, when they are real, are equally effective, let me quote briefly a college student's reaction, in a different course:

> Your sense of humour in the class was cheering: we all felt relaxed because you showed us your human self, not a mechanical teacher image. I feel as if I have more understanding and faith in my teachers now. I feel closer to the students too.

Another student in the same course:

> It wasn't as if there was a teacher in the class, but rather someone whom we could trust and identify as a 'sharer.' You were so perceptive and sensitive to our thoughts, and this made it all the more 'authentic' for me. It was an 'authentic' experience, not just a class.

I trust I am making it clear that to be real is not always easy, nor is it achieved all at once, but it is basic to the person who wants to become that revolutionary individual, a facilitator of learning.

Prizing, acceptance, trust

There is another attitude that stands out in those who are successful in facilitating learning. I have observed this attitude. I have experienced it. Yet, it is hard to know what term to put to it so I shall use several. I think of it as prizing the learner, prizing her feelings, her opinions, her person. It is a caring for the learner, but a nonpossessive caring. It is an acceptance of this other individual as a separate person, having worth in her own right. It is a bsic trust—a belief that this other person is somehow fundamentally trustworthy. Whether we call it prizing, acceptance, trust, or by some other term, it shows up a variety of observable ways. The facilitator who has a considerable degree of this attitude can be fully acceptant of the fear and hesitation of the student as she approaches a new problem as well as acceptant of the pupil's satisfaction in achivement. Such a teacher can accept the student's occasional apathy, her erratic desires to explore byroads of knowledge, as well as her disciplined efforts to achieve major goals. She can accept personal feelings that both disturb and promote learning — rivalry with a sibling, hatred of authority, concern about personal adequacy. What we are describing is a prizing of the learner as an imperfect human being with many feelings, many potentialities. The facilitator's prizing or acceptance of the learner is an operational expression of her essential confidence and trust in the capacity of the human organism.

I would like to give some examples of this attitude from the classroom situation. Here any teacher statements would be properly suspect since many of us would like to feel we hold such attitudes and might have a biased perception of our qualities. But let me indicate how this attitude of prizing, of accepting, of trusting appears to the student who is fortunate enough to experience it.

Here is a statement from a college student in a class with Dr. Morey Appel.

> Important, mature, and capable of doings thingk on my own. I want to think for myself and this need cannot be accomplished through text books and lectures alone, but through living. I thing you see me as a person with real feelings and needs, an individual. What I say and do are significant expressions from me, and you recognize this.

The facilitator who cares, who prizes, who trusts the learner creates a climate for learning so different from the ordinary classroom that any resemblance is purely coincidental.

Empathic understanding

A further element that establishes a climate for self-initiated, experiential learning is empathic understanding. When the teacher has the ability to understand the student's reactions from the inside, has a sensitive awareness of the way the process of education and learning seems to the student, then again the likelihood of significant learnig is increased.

This kind of understanding is sharply different from the usual evaluative understanding, which follows the pattern of 'I understand what is wrong with you.' When there is a sensitive empathy, however, the reaction in the learner follows something of this pattern, 'At last someone understands how it feels and seems to be me without wanting to analyse me or judge me. Now I can blossom and grow and learn.'

This attitude of standing in the other's shoes, of viewing the world through the student's eyes, is almost unheard of in he classroom. One could listen to thousands of ordinary classroom interactions without coming across one instance of clearly communicated, sensitively accurate, emphatic understanding. But it has a tremendously releasing effect when it occurs.

Let me take an illustration from Virginia Axline, dealing with a second grade boy. Jay, age 7, has been aggressive, a trouble-maker, slow of speech and learning. Because of his 'cussing', he was taken to the principal, who paddled him, unknown to Miss Axline. During a free work period, Jay fashioned very carefully a man of clay down to a hat and a handkerchief in his pocket. 'Who is that?' asked Miss Axline. 'Dunno,' replied Jay. 'Maybe it is the principal. He has a handkerchief in his pocket like that.' Jay glared at the clay figure. 'Yes,' he said. Then he began to tear the head off and looked up and smiled. Miss Axline said, 'You sometimes feel like twisting his head off, don't you? You get so mad at him.' Jay tore off one arm, another, then beat the figure to a pulp with his fists. Another boy, with the perception of the young, explained, 'Jay is mad at Mr X because he licked him this noon.' 'Then you must feel lots better now,' Miss Axline commented. Jay grinned and began to rebuild Mr X.

The other examples I have cited also indicate how deeply appreciative students feel when they are simply understood - not evaluated, not judged, simply understood from their own point of view, not the teacher's. If any teacher set herself the task of endeavouring to make one non-evaluative, acceptant, empathic response per day to a student's demonstrated or verbalized feeling, I believe she would discover the potency of this currrently almost none existent kind of understanding.

What are the bases of facilitative attitudes?

A 'puzzlement'

It is natural that we do not always have attitudes I have been describing. Some teachers raise the question, 'But what if I am not feeling empathic, do not, at this moment, prize or accept or like my students. What then?' My response is that realness is the most important of the attitudes mentioned, and it is not accidental that this attitude was described first. So if one has little understanding of the student's inner world and a dislike for the students or their behaviour, it is almost certainly more constructive to be real than to be pseudoempathic or to put on a facade of caring.

But this is not nearly as simple as it sounds. To be genuine, or honest, or congruent, or real means to be this way about oneself. I cannot be real about another because I do not know what is real for him. I can only tell, if I wish to be truly honest, what is going on in me.

Let me take an example. Early in this chapter I reported Miss Shiel's feelings about the 'mess' created by the art work. Essentially she said, 'I find it maddening to live with the mess! I'm neat and orderly and it is driving me to distraction.' But suppose her feelings had come out some what differently in the disguised way that is much more common in classrooms at all levels. She might have said, 'You are the messiest children I've ever seen! You don't care about tidiness or cleanliness. You are just terrible!' This is most definitely not an example of genuineness or realness, in the sense in which I am using these terms. There is profound distinction between the two statements, which I should like to spell out.

In the second statement she is telling nothing of herself, sharing none of her feelings. Doubtless the children will sense that she is angry, but because children are perceptively shrewd, they may be uncertain as to whether she is angry at them or has just come from an argument with the principal. It has none of the honesty of the first statement in which she tells of her own upsetness, of her own feeling of being driven to distraction.

Another aspect of the second statement is that it is all made up of judgements or evaluations, and like most judgements, they are all arguable. Are these children messy, or are they simply excited and involved in what they are doing? Do they care nothing about tidiness, or is it simply they don't care about it every day? If a group of visitors were coming, would their attitude be different? Are they terrible, or simply children? I trust it is evident that when we make jedgements, they are almost never fully accurate and hence cause resentment and anger as well as guilt and apprehension. Had she used the second statement, the response of the class would have been entirely different.

I am going to some lengths to clarify this point because I have found from experience that to stress the value of being real, of being one's feelings, is taken by some as a licence to pass judgements on others, to project on others all the feelings that one should be 'owning'. Nothing could be further from my meaning.

Actually the achievement of realness is most difficult, and even when one wishes to be truly genuine, it occurs but rarely. Certainly it is not simply a matter of the words used, and if one iss feeling judgemental, the use of a verbal formula that sounds like the sharing of feelings will not help. It is just another instance of a facade, of a lack of genuineness. Only slowly can we learn to be truly real. For first of all, one must be close to one's feelings, capable of being aware of them. Then one must be willing to take the risk of sharing them as they are, inside, not disguising them as judgements, or attributing them to other people. This is why I so admire Miss Shiel's sharing of her anger and frustration, without in any way disguising it.

A trust in the human organism.

It would be most unlikely that one could hold the three attitudes I have described, or could commit herself to being a facilitator of learning unless she has come to have a profound trust in the human organism and its potentialities. If I distrust the human being, then I must cram her with information of my own choosing lest she go her own mistaken way. But if I trust the capacity of the human individual for developing her own petentiality, then I can provide her with many opportunities and permit her to choose her own way and her own direction in her learning.

It is clear I believe, that the teachers rely basically upon the tendency towards fulfilment, towards actualization, in their students. They are basing their work on the hypothesis that students who are in real contact with problems that are relevant to them wish to learn, want to grow, seek to discover, endeavour to master, desire to create, move towards self descipline. The teacher is attempting to develop a quality of climate in the classroom and quality of personal relationship with students that will permit these natural tendencies to come to their fruition.

Living the uncertainty of discovery

I believe it should be said that this basically confident view of the human being and the attitudes toward students that I have described do not appear suddenly, in some miraculous manner, in the facilitator of learning. Instead, they come about through taking risks, through acting on tentative hypotheses. I can only state that I started my career with the firm view that individuals must be manipulated for their own good; I only came to the attitudes I have described and the trust in the individual that is implicit in them because I found that these attitudes were so much more potent in producing learning and constructive change. Hence, I believe that it is only by risking herself in these new ways that the teacher can discover, for herself, whether or not they are effective, whether or not they are for her.

I will then draw a conclusion, based on the experiences of the several facilitators and their students that have been included up to this point: When a facilitator creates, even to a modest degree, a classroom climate characterized by all that she can achieve of realness, prizing, and empathy; when she trusts the constructive tendency of the individual and the group; then she discovers that she has inaugurated an educational revolution. Learning of a different quality, proceeding at a different pace, with a greater degree of pervasiveness, occurs. Feelings - positive, negative, confused - become a part of the classroom experience. Learning becomes life and a very vital life at that. The student is on the way, sometimes excitedly, sometimes reluctantly, to becoming a learning, changing being.

Evidence from students

Certainly before the research evidence was in, students were making it clear by their reactions to student-centred or person centred classrooms that an educational revolution was underway. This kind of evidence persists to the present day.

The most striking learnings of students

exposed to such a climate are by no means restricted to greater achievement in the three Rs. The significant learnings are the more personal ones - independence, self-initiated and the responsible learning, release of creativity, a tendency to become more of a person. I can only illustrate this by picking, almost at random, statements from students whose teachers have endeavoured to create a climate of trust, of prizing, of realness, of understanding, and above all, of freedom here is one of a number of statements made by students in a course on poetry led by Dr. Samuel Moon.

In retrospect, I find that I have actually enjoyed this course, both as a class and as an experiment, although it had me quite unsettled at times. This, in itself, make the course worthwhile since the majority of my courses this semester merely had me bored with them and the whole process of 'higher education.' Quite aside from anything else, due mostly to this course, I found myself devoting more time to writing poetry than to writing short stories, which temporarily interfered with my writing class.

I should like to point out one very definite thing which I have gained from the course; this is an increased readiness on my part to listen to and to seriously consider the opinions of my fellow students. In view of my past attitude, this alone makes the course valuable. I suppose the real result of any course can be expressed in answer to the question, 'Would you take it over again?' My answer would be an unqualified 'Yes.'

I should like to add to this several comments from Dr. Bull's sophomore students in a class in adolescent psychology. The first two are midsemester comments.

This course is proving to be vital and profound experience for me... This unique learning situation is giving me a whole new conception of just what learning is...I am experiencing a real growth in this atmosphere of constructive freedom... the whole experience is challenging.

I feel that the course had been of great value to me... I'm glad to have had this experience because it has made me think... I've never been so personally involved with a course before, especially outside the classroom. It has been frustrating, rewarding, enjoyable, and tiring!

The other comments are from the end of the course:

This course is not ending with the close of the semester for me, but continuing... I don't know of any greater benefit which can be gained from a course than this desire for further knowledge.

I feel as though this type of class situation has stimulated me more in making me realize where my responsibilities lie, especially as far as doing required work on my own. I no longer feel as though a test date is the criterion for rreading a book. I feel as though my future work will be done for what I will get out of it, not just for a test mark.

I think that more I am acutely aware of the

breakdown in communications that does exist in our society from seeing what happened in our class ... I've grown immensely. I know that I am a different person than I was when I came into that class... It has done a great deal in helping me understand myself better ... thank you for contributing to my growth.

My idea of education has been to gain information from the teacher by attending lectures. The emphasis and focus were on the teacher ... One of the biggest changes that I experienced in this class was my outlook on education. Learning is something more than a grade on a report card. No one can measure what you have learned because it's personal thing. I was very confused between learning and memorization. I could memorize very well, but I doubt if I ever learned as much as I could have. I believe my attitude toward learning has changed from a grade-centred outlook to a more personal one.

If you wish to know what this type of course seems like to a sixth grader, let me give you a sampling of the reactions of Miss Shiel's youngsters, misspelling and all.

I feel that I am learning self ability. I am learning not only work but I am learning that you can learn on your own as well as someone and all.

I like this plan because there is a lot of freedom. I also learn more this way than the other way you don't have to wait for others you can go at your own speed rate and it also takes a lot of responsibility.

Or let me take two more, from Dr. Appell's graduate class:

I have been thinking about what happened through this experience. The only conclusion I come to is that if I try to measure what is going on, or what I was at the beginning, I have got to know what I was when I started - and I don't...so many things I did and feel are just lost...scrambled up inside... They don't seem to come out in a nice little pattern or organization I can say and write...There are so many things left unsaid. I know I have only scratched the surface, I guess. I can feel so many things almost ready to come out... maybe that's enough. It seems all kinds of things have so much more meaning now than ever before...This experience has had meaning, has done things to me and I am not sure how much or how far just yet. I think I am going to be a better me in the fall. That's one thing I am sure of.

You follow no play, yet I'm learning. Since the term began I seem to feel more alive, more real to myself. I enjoy being alone as well as with other people. My relationships with children and other adults are becoming more emotional and involved. Eating an orange last week, I peeled the skin off each separate orange section and liked it better with the transparent shell off. It was juicier and fresher tasting that way. I began to think, that's how I feel sometimes, without a transparent wall around me, really cimmunicating my feelings. I feel that I'm growing how much, I don't know. I'm thinking, considering, pondering and learning.

I can't read these student statements - sixth grade, college, graduate level- without being deeply moved. Here are teachers, risking themselves, being themselves, trusting their students, adventuring into the existential unknown, taking the subjective leap. And what happens? Exciting, incredible human events. You can sense persons being created, learnings being initiated, future citizens rising to meet the challenge of unknown worlds. If only one teacher out of 100 dared to risk, dared to be, dared to trust, dared to understand, we would have an infusion of living spirit into education that would, in my estimation, be priceless.

The effect upon the instructor

Let me turn to another dimension that excites me. I have spoken of the effect upon the student of a climate that encourages significant, self-reliant, personal learning. But I have said nothing about the reciprocal effect upon the instructor. When she has been the agent for the release of such self-initiated learning, the faculty member finds herself changed as well as her student. One such says:

To say that I am overwhelmed by what happened only faintly reflects my feelings. I have taught for many years but I have never experienced anything remotely resembling what occurred. I, for my part, never found in a classroom so much of the whole person coming forth, so deeply involved, so deeply stirred. Further, I question if in the traditional setup, with its emphasis on subject matter, examinations, grades, there is or there can be place for the 'becoming' person with his deep and manrfold needs as he struggles to fulfil himself. But this is going far afield. I can only report to you what happened and to say that I am grateful and that I am also humbled by the experience. I would like you to know this for it has enriched my life and being.

Another faculty member reports as follows:

Rogers has said that relationships conducted on these assumptions mean 'turning presentn day education upside down.' I have found this to be true as I have tried to implement this way of living with students. The experiences I have had have plunged me into relationships which have been significant and challenging and beyond compare for me. They have inspired me and stimulated me and left me at times shaken and awed with their consequences for both me and the students. They have led me to the fact of what I can only call...the tragedy of education in our time - student after student who reports this to be his first experience with total trust, with freedom to be and to move in ways most consistent for the enhancement and maintenance of the core of dignity which somehow has survived humiliation, distortion, and corrosive cynicism.

Too idealistic?

Some readers may feel that the whole approach of this chapter—the belief that teachers can relate as persons to their students - is hopelessly unrealistic and idealistic. They may see that in essence it is encouraging both teachers and students to be creative in their relationship to each other and in their relationship to subject matter, and feel that such a goal is quite impossible. They are not alone in this. I have heard scientists at leading schools of science and scholars in leading universities arguing that it is absurd to try to encourage all students to be creative—we need hosts of mediocre technicians and workers, and if a few creative scientists and artists and leaders emerge, that will be enough. That may be enough for them. It may be enough to suit you. I want to go on record as saying it is not enough to suit me. When I realize the incredible potential in the ordinary student, I want to try to release it. We are working hard to rethe nucleus of the atom. If we do not devote equal energy—yes, and equal money-to the release of the potential of the individual person then the enormous discrepancy between our level of physical enefgy resources and human energy resources will doom us to a deserved and universal destruction.

10 Toward Guidelines for Good Practice

Specifying criteria

I want to present an evaluative rationale that readers can adopt, perhaps partially, perhaps wholly, to guide their evaluations. The rationale is derived from my philosophy of adult education, and it is a brief elaboration of this philosophy that ends my book. The critical evaluative rationale, therefore, is based on the extent to which certain philosophical dimensions are evident in the facilitation of adult learning. Briefly stated, this critical philosophy regards the facilitation of learning as a value-laden activity in which curricular and programmatic choices reflect normative preferences. It sees adult education as a socialization agent of some force, capable of confirming values and behaviors uncritically assimilated in earlier periods or of prompting adults to challenge the validity of their received ideas and codes.

Developing in adults a sense of their personal power and self-worth is seen as a fundamental purpose of all education and training efforts. Only if such a sense of individual empowerment is realized will adults possess the emotional strength to challenge behaviours, values, and beliefs accepted uncritically by a majority. Both causally antecedent to, and concurrent with, this developing sense of self-worth in the individual comes an awareness of the contextuality of knowledge and beliefs. The task of the educator, then, becomes that of encouraging adults to perceive the relative, contextual nature of previously unquestioned givens. Additionally, the educator should assist the adult to reflect on the manner in which values, beliefs, and bahaviours previously deemed unchallengable can be critically analyzed. Through presenting alternative ways of interpreting and creating the world to adults, the educator fosters a willingness to consider alternative ways of living.

These criteria are offered for consideration by educators as fundamental indicators by which they may judge the worth of a formal or informal effort to facilitate learning. In real life, of course, all adult will not develop a sense of self-worth, an awareness of the contextuality of knowledge, a willingness to speculate on alternatives, and a capacity to re-create their personal and social worlds, according to the neatly sequenced stages described in the previous paragraph. Some adults will come to appreciate the contextuality of knowledge or learn to speculate on alternatives, without having the sense of self-worth and personal power needed to realize those alternatives. Others will have the internal strength to alter certain peripheral features of their lives but will be unable to change the patterns that govern their significant personal relationships. Still others may consider social alternatives and even imagine new political forms, but lack the techniques, skills, or collective support needed to effect change. This does not mean, however, that we should abandon attempts to specify as clearly as possible the criteria we are adopting to determine the success of our efforts.

Such criteria will inevitably, take the form of abstractions. They will be oversimplifications of reality. The real world of social encounters is sufficiently chaotic to make the detection of whether or not these criteria have been satisfied a correspondingly haphazard and often messy enterprise. Nevertheless if we make no attempt to specify criteria, we will be unable to assign value and worthwhileness to different activities. All educational encounters will then exist in some kind of moral vacuum, and we will be unable to judge whether a lecture in which a religious or political dogma is fervently and uncritically expounded is more or less educational than a discussion of the ethical assumptions underlying communism and capitalism.

If we are to wear the mantle of "educator," we must, at some minimum level, make explicit the criteria by which we determine the educational worth of our efforts. Not to do so is unthinking or dishonest, and it is to consign ourselves to being adaptive and reactive satisfiers of whatever consumer learning needs happen to capture our attention. But it is to the means for determining whether or not these criteria are actually being met in an educational activity that we must now turn our attention.

The preceding chapters have been concerned chiefly with matters of practice-facilitating adult learning through self directed modes, using and ragogical methods, teaching adults through discussion groups, developing programs for adult learners, and evaluating effective practice. Implicit in these discussion of practice, however, has been a concept of facilitation somewhat different from that held by many practitioners. In this final chapter it is important that the philosophical assumptions on which this concept is based be stated clearly. As has been repeatedly argued, practical expertise that exist in a moral vacuum can be a dangerous thing. Practitioners can become technically proficient but find that without a firm philosophical rationale to guide the application of their skills, they are devoting their efforts to programs and purpose that are morally dubious.

Contained in these characteristics are features that will be familiar to those who know the literature of humanistic psychology and psychotherapy- a respect for participants in the teaching-learning transaction, a commitment to collaborative modes of program development, and an acknowledgment of the educational value of life experiences.

Hence, effective facilitation means that learners will be challenged to examine their previously held values, beliefs, and behaviors and will be confronted with ones that they may not wnat to consider. Such challenges and confrontations need not be done in an adversarial, combative, or threatening manner; indeed, the most effective facilitator is one who can encourage adults to consider rationally and carefully perspectives and interpretations of the world that diverage from those they already hold, without making these adults feel they are being cajoled or threatened. This experience may produce anxiety, but such anxiety should be accepted as a normal component of learning and not as something to be avoided at all costs for fear that learners will leave the group. There are forms of fulfillment that are quite unlike those produced by a wholly joyful encounter with a new form of knowledge of a new skill area. It is this dimension of increased insight through critical reflection on current assumptions and past beliefs and behaviors that is sometimes ignored in treatments of adult learning. One purpose of this book is to place the prompting of this form of learning at the heart of what it means to be a good facilitator.

It is important to state, however, that because teaching learning transactions are collaborative, the prompting of critical reflection may not always be done by the participant designated as the facilitator. In the most effective learning groups, facilitating behaviors are assumed by various members of these groups at different times. One features the leaderless groups discussed in Chapter Six—women's consciousness-raising groups, quality circles, political advocacy groups, and so on—is that the member who is responsible for the initial formation of these groups does not have to assume full responsibility for facilitating learning. As a group culture develops, various members will challenge others to examine their current ways of thinking and living, and this activity will be seen as wholly appropriate. As a recent study of self-concept change among black women students at college points out, one of the valued characteristics of good facilitators as identified by these women is a readiness to challenge learners.

Building a critical philosophy of practice

The public articulation of a philosophy of effective practice is an activity viewed with apparent indifference or distaste by many educators and trainers of adults. Such educators might appear to an outsider to be bereft of any rationale for their practice. This is rarely the case. In reality, most practitioners accept employing agency mission statements as general definitions of purpose or declare good practice to be the satisfaction of felt and expressed needs. These positions in themselves exemplify a philosophical rationale-that of pragmatism.

Acceptance of this pragmatic rationale is perhaps most evident in the tendency to equate the design of effective program-planning models with the sum total of effective practice. According to this argument, the education of adults is a matter of designing, conducting, and evaluating educational experiences so as to meet the felt needs of adults. Hence, practitioner effectiveness becomes defined in terms of processes and activities-the ability to design, conduct, and evaluate programs for learners-rather than in terms of fundamental purposes or curriculum. But if we view effective practice solely as the improvement of ever more refined practice skills and regard facilitator roles and responsibilities as being primarily those of technicians of design, we denude practice of any philosophical rationale, future orientation, or purposeful mission. There exists no philosophical yardstick in terms of criteria of success, notions of purpose, or appropriate curricula against which the effectiveness of such facilitation can be judged. Furthermore, if we accept the view that we should serve only felt needs, then our priorities, purposes, and primary functions will be wholly determined by others. Our curriculum will be devised in response to demands made by those who can best attract our attention and are most articulate in presenting their case.

To counter this danger that facilitation will become solely a responsive, reactive activity, it is important that practitioners develop a philosophical rationale, or what Apps calls a belief system, to grant their practice order and purpose. They need to identify those characteristics by which the fundamental worth of any attempt to facilitate adult learning can be judged.

This does not mean that such a philosophy must be exemplified to its fullest degree in every educational encounter with adults. Such an insistence would be so intimidating to practitioners as to prevent any attempt to implement a philosophy. We should regard this rationale rather as a variable that can be realized to a greater or lesser extent at different times, in different settings, with different groups. Even within one class session the extent to which this philosophy is realized will vary with the nature of the individuals concerned, the exercises pursued, and the educator's conduct. Nonetheless, it is vital that a clear rationale be articulated so that practitioners may have a benchmark for judging the extent to which their activities exemplify fundamental purposes, principles, and practice. Without a coherent rationale, practice will be condemned to an adaptive, reactive mode. Practitioner activities will be determined by current curricular trends or by the ability of certain individuals and groups to make themselves heard and their demands felt.

Several writers have indeed warned of the dangers of succumbing to a reactive and pragmatic rationale. Lawson and Monette have both condemned the insidious influence of the service rationale on programs for adult learners. According to this rationale, practitioners are technicians whose function is to cater to the expressed needs of their clients in as effective a manner as possible. These writers point out that by responding to felt needs, the educator does not have to make value judgments concerning the relative merits of different curricular offerings. Only rarely is there any acknowledgment in the literature of the moral and professional requirement that the educator act in accordance with value choices.

Crabtree has also condemned the manner in which the idea of "customer service" comes to determine the form of the curriculum for adult learners. Similarly, Powell warned against the importing of a business rationale into adult education and expressed his concern at the growing tendency to let a preoccupation with needs assessments and marketing procedures replace the setting of fundamental goals for a program. Seduction of the programmer by evidence of a strong and immediate demand for a certain course offering was also recognized by Herring, who blamed the galloping mediocrity he saw in many programs for adult learners on the institutionally prescribed need to increase enrollments. Herring lamented the tendency of program planners to avoid social and political issues that they thought were too serious or too contentious to draw large numbers of participants.

In adult education, however, we seem currently to be in danger of becoming preoccupied with refining techniques to the exclusion of any consideration of the rationale underlying those techniques. We are philosophically numb, concerned with the design of ever more sophisticated needs assessment techniques, program planning models, and evaluative procedures. It seems not to have occurred to us that the perfection of technique can only be meaningful when placed within a context of some fundamental human or social purpose. Technique is, after all, only a means to broader ends. When technique is worshipped to the exclusion of the human or social purposes it is meant to serve, then it is easy for us to become dazzled by the convolutions of the latest shaman of procedure and by the pronouncements of those who flaunt commonsense ideas regarding teaching and learning under the guise of presenting a revolutionary paradigm of practice.

In contrast, this chapter attempts to comment on the fundamental nature and proper purpose of facilitating learning by outlining a philosophy of practice that comprises three fundamental elements. Finally, on the basis of this definition and its general statement of purpose there should be formulated a set of criteria by which the success of various practitioner efforts can be judged. Such criteria would allow us to reflect on our own practice and to examine the activities of others in terms of their effectiveness.

This definition, statement of purposes, and explication of criteria should be firmly and avowedly prescriptive. A philosophy of practice should, at the most fundamental level, be concerned with the resolution of second-order questions, that is questions that cannot be answered by recourse to the empirical world. In other words, we cannot conduct a survey to determine in some objectively empirical sense what should be the purpose of our efforts. We can conduct assessments of present levels of competence and declare certain populations to be in states of educational need with regard to some previously defined standard. Such assessments are only objective, however, to the extent that they are based on a normatively defined standard of competence. Similarly, by conducting a Delphi survey of adult education professors, we can determine their views on the proper purposes of facilitation. This survey will not answer for us, however, the fundamental question concerning what should be the purpose of educating adults, for this is a question that is explored in a quite separate area of intellectual discourse. The domain of discourse surrounding such a question is one of prescriptive preferences, moral commitments, and categorical imperatives. We will come to construct our philosophy of practice on the basis of the personal and social imperatives we feel to be most potent. In the course of this construction we will admittedly be cognizant of the opinions of those intellectual leaders we respect. Such opinions cannot grant to our philosophy its internal power and commitment, however, since this will be derived from our experience of the world and from our personal belief system concerning the most desirable and meaningful aspects of this experience.

Implementing the rationale

A philosophy of practice should allow considerable scope for operationalization. In an activity such as facilitating learning, statements of fundamental purpose are of limited value if they cannot be realized in terms of practice. Concomitant with this outline of a philosophical rationale, therefore, should be some guidance in regard to teaching method, curriculum development, program planning, and evaluation. But such techniques will not exist in their own right; they will be grounded in, and derived from, a carefully explicated rationale. This rationale from which are derived various practical injunctions in terms of planning, teaching, curriculum development, and evaluation - will serve as a yardstick against which the effectiveness and worth of a particular effort can be judged. This philosophy and its concomitant operationalizations should serve as a benchmark and as a guide by which practice can be mapped.

The philosophy of practice proposed within this last chapter centers on the notion of the adult's developing sense of control and autonomy. Such autonomy is not to be equated with atomistic isolation; rather, it is realized in personal relationships, in sociopolitical behavior, and in intellectual judgment. The purpose of facilitation is to assist individuals to begin to exercise control over their own lives, their interpersonal relationships, and the social forms and structures within which they live. This is not to say that facilitation will enable adults to exert complete control over all aspects of their worlds. However, it is possible to envisage existences that are more or less meaningful and authentic to the individuals involved, according to the degree to which they feel they have some proactive role in creating their worlds.

It is proposed that all involved in teaching-learning transactions assist each other to identify the exernal sources and internalized assumptions framing their conduct and to be ready to assess these critically. Such critical awareness will involve an appreciation of the contextual, provisional, and relative nature of truth, public knowledge, and personal beliefs. When a disjunction becomes evident between adults' individual aspirations and the socially received codes, value frameworks, and belief systems informing their behavior, then autonomy is reflected in a jettisoning of received assumptions. Occurring along with this abandonment of assumptions perceived as irrelevant and inauthentic will be the transformation of individual and collective circumstances.

Teaching-learning transactions are no exceptions to this rule; indeed they possess an unusual degree of potency in that the facilitator's statements and comments are typically granted a high degree of credibility and significance by learners. Learners grant authority to interpretations, generalizations, and statements of preference made by the facilitator, even though he or she may arow this equality of status with learners and emphasize that they are partners in a collaborative endeavour. Facilitators may profoundly dislike this role, particularly those of a democratic, egalitarian temper. To be the beneficiary of imputations of moral as well as intellectual superiority by learners is confining and often even embarrassing. However, inasmuch as most adults received an initial education that encouraged them to see teachers as authority figures, it is hardly surprising if they prove incapable, at least at first, of viewing the facilitator as partner and intellectual collaborator.

This ascribed authority places facilitators in an uncomfortable position, particularly if they subscribe to andragogical principles. It also makes the adoption of an ethical code of practice-a requirement of first importance in any profession doubly necessary. Any position of authority, whether ascribed or prescribed, carries within it the possibility of abuse. This potential will be reduced if facilitators seek, as rigorously as possible, to submit all assertions to critical scrutiny. Facilitators will cite apporopriate evidence for any generalizations they make and will treat all theories, explanatory systems, standards of esthetic discriminations, conceptual constructs, and criteria of excellence as provisional and relative.

Aside from viewing theoretical systems or explanations as provisional, the ficilitator should also present alternative interpretations and possibilities to students. Such alternatives may be esthetic, cognitive, or sociopolitical. Hence, a course on craft skills should encourage inquiries into the origins of standards of excellence and not concentrate only on the development of psychomotor skills exemplifying those standards. A similar requirement also holds for courses dealing with bodies of cognitive knowledge. These should submit central concepts and theoretical frameworks to critical review. Criteria of intellectual excellence should be viewed as humanly contrived, not divinely ordained, and all statements and assertions should be regarded as provisional. With regard to those courses dealing with behavioral phenomena-for example, role training, interpersonal skill development, or counselling techniques-the twin canons of relativity and provisionality also pertain.

In fields such as health education, administrative studies, or personnel management, training courses can only qualify as examples of effective facilitation if the behavioral paradigms presented in them are subjected to critical scrutiny. Moreover, if such courses are to be seen as involving education and not simply training, they must incorporate a willingness to consider alternatives to the popularly prevailing norms governing correct professional behaviors. Participants in such courses would learn to be skeptical of definitive sets of principles of practice and to view conventionally accepted wisdom or apparently exemplary behaviors as relative and provisional.

The chief argument proposed here is that effective facilitation is present when adults come to appreciate the relative, provisional, and contextual nature of public and private knowledge and when they come to understand that the belief systems, value frameworks, and moral codes informing their conduct are culturally constructed. It is also evident when adults are enabled to create meaning to their personal worlds through a continual redefinition of their relationships with others. Following on from this exhibition of personal autonomy and the realization that individual circumstances can be consciously altered comes the insight that it is possible, in concert with others, to change cultural forms, including attitudinal sets, role expectations, conventions, and folkways, as well as social structures.

This concept of facilitation is obviously prescriptive; that is to say, the outcomes identified in the preceding paragraph are given in the form of stipulative preference statements. This is not to imply that adults can become adept at critical reflectivity in some final, static manner. Rather, it is to say that adults should be encouraged to engage in the continuous critical analysis of received assumptions, commonsense knowledge, and conventional behaviors. The state of adulthood can never be fully realized, and it is not a question of an adult's acquiring a set of fixed competencies. Adult education as a transactional encounter is essentially a process. Central to this process is a continual scrutiny by all involved of the conditions that have shaped their private and public worlds, combined with a continuing attempt to reconstruct those worlds. This praxis of continual reflection and action might be accurately viewed as a process of lifelong learning.

It is important to realize that philosophical prescriptions painstakingly derived from impeccably developed rationales are going to be contradicted daily in the real world of practice.

Teaching-learning transactions are, after all, dynamic interactions—psychosocial dramas in which unforeseen eventualities, serendipitious circumstances, and individual idiosyncrasies constantly distort our neatly planned visions of how our learning groups should function. Educators employed within formal educational institutions daily contradict their own prescriptions concerning how best to foster learners' freedom and individuality.

An example drawn from my own practive may illustrate what I mean. In a course I teach on the philosophy and theory of adult educations, I generally invite groups members to identify within this same course any elements of "banking education" practices that they may perceive. Very often, as the learning group reviews the curriculum, format of meetings, and evaluative procedures of the last few weeks or months, it becomes evident that a familiar dynamic has operated, despite all our best intentions to the contrary. According to this dynamic, I have begun by emphasizing the collaborative nature of the course and then, with the apparently unwitting connivance of course members, have proceeded to assume major responsibility for the most important decisions concerning course content and format. Although all members of the group pay frequent testimony to the need to draw on individual participants' own experiences, to ground curricula in their concerns, and to evolve a collaborative format, we fall easily and unthinkingly into a pattern of interaction whereby I begin to expound on adult education from an expert standpoint and they passively receive my distilled wisdom. Participants and I have been socialized to such an extent into a banking education mode that we fall easily into our respective roles of authority figure and inexperienced learners, no matter what our resolutions to the contrary. Educators of adults, as much as learners, uncritically assimilate various assumptions, norms, beliefs, and values, and it is a genuinely humbling experience to ask participants in a learning group to point out the disguised authoritarianism in one's own practice.

What must never be lost sight of, however, is the need to develop a clear rationale for practice, even though that rationale may be contradicted or only partially realized in the day-to-day practitioner reality of facilitating learning. Without such a rationale we are little more than reactive automatons-ciphers through whom are channeled the latest curricular or methodological fads, irrespective of any consideration of their innate validity. While a healthy skepticism regarding the possibility of continually exemplifying such a philosophy of practice is essential to the sanity of facilitators, the necessity to develop such a philosophy should be regarded as fundamental to good practice.

Educators of adults have grown accustomed to living with organizational and professional contradictions. They probably became facilitators because they saw that as a way of increasing individuals' fulfillment, happiness, and sense of control, yet organizational criteria for their success are frequently antithetical to these motivations. In colleges and universities, for example, educators are encouraged to develop curricula and to arrange classrooms so as to attract the largest possible number of learners. The reason for this is not only to add to the sum total of human happiness and enlightenment, but also to make money. Educational institutions, particulary in an era dominated by supply side economics, are viewed by politicians, trustees, administrators, and sometimes even faculty partly as educational enterprises partly as business operations. Hence, the greater the numbers of students that can be attracted, the greater the revenues for the educational institution. In business and industrial settings, these economic criteria are applied quite openly to determining the success of training initiatives. While trainers may hope that workshops and seminars will enable adults to make sense of themselves and their worlds, their success as trainers will be judged by whether or not productivity rises as a consequence of attendance at the training sessions.

Furthermore, most educators and trainers of adults subscribe to a professional code that acknowledges the value of democratic collaboration and the inequity of forcing students to learn. Yet in their daily practice they repeatedly encounter a set of contextual constraints that force them into precisely the behaviors that they criticize in philosophical terms. Institutional timetables, economic necessities, standardized curricula, and unofficial norms of "what works in the real world" all conspire to nudge the educator into more didactic authoritarian attitudes and behaviors than he or she might wish. The conspiracy of contextual constraints becomes all the more compelling when learners repeatedly declare that they wish for more direction from facilitators or that they want facilitators to "put more of themselves" into the learning encounter. Learners, as much as facilitators, have been socialized into a view of education as an authoritarian-based transmission of information, skills, and attitudinal sets from teacher to taught. Under these circumstances, it will often be hard for educators to stand firm against the temptation to take more control over the learning encounter. Yet to give in to this temptation is to reaffirm precisely those patterns of dependency that prevent adults from becoming empowered, self-directed learners.

Given the force of these organizational constraints and professional expectations, it is not surprising that facilitators revert, with only an occasional twinge of conscience, to patterns of behavior they observed in their own teachers. How, then, can they break these patterns and begin to assume the kinds of facilitation roles outlined in this book? My answer is, only by developing a thoughtful rationale to guide their practice. Possessed of such a rationale, facilitators are more likely to stand firm against organizational and professional imperatives that exert pressure on them to dominate learners under the guise of "providing structure' or 'clarifying ambiguities." Without such a rationale it is likely that most facilitators will sooner or later fall unthinkingly into patterns of facilitation that support structures of organizational convenience and confirm learners' patterns of dependency learned in the school classroom but have little to do with assisting adults to create, and re-create, their personal, occupational, and political worlds.

Central to the nation of discussion are two features that may be either complementary or contradictory. Discussion sessions can be judged successful to the extent to which they purssure certain cognitive ends or to the extent to which all members offer verbal contributions of approximately equal length. In a critique of discussion behaviors, I have examined the way in which discussion groups can become arenas of psychodynamic struggle and fields of emotional battle. Many adults were schooled in competitive settings in which the pursuit of knowledge was obscured by the quest for grades and examination success. It is hard for such individuals to accept openness of discourse and to tolerate diverse opinions. Since discussion session are invested with emotional significance, any disagreement may well be interpreted as a personal assualt. Additionally, groups tend to place high value on cohesiveness and to exclude deviant opinions. But as Fawett-Hill maintains, it is important that groups tolerate deviant opinions. Such divergence guards against intellectual stasis.

Bridges has specified certain epistemological underpinnings of discussion. All members should have respect for each other, and all should be septical of their own, as well as of others', authority. Bridge also prescribes a moral culture for group discussion; it includes six ethical principles that participants should accept as the tacit assumptions underlying their discourse: reasonableness, peaceable orderliness, truthfulness, freedom, equality, and respect for persons. Discussion conforming to the epistemological principles and moral culture outlined by Bridges would be characterized by openness of content, membership, and learning outcomes. Participants would set aside their own prejudices to entertain imaginative speculation.

Paterson proposes discussion as the educational activity par excellence. It is an educational end it itself, erquiring no extrinsic justification. To Paterson, adults commit and discover their whole beings in the process of presenting for group consideration their interpretations of their experience. He writes that "to adress others in discussion...is to bear witness to one's attempt to reconstruct ones, experience meaningfully, and it is at the same time to invite others to share this reconstructed experience". In this way participation in open discussion becomes a characteristically human activity of the most intimate and fundamental kind. Since openness is an essential characteristic for discussion, the concept of guided discussion must be discarded. In Paterson's words, "True discussion cannot be directed, or even guided, for to attempt to do so is in effect to opt out of the discussion, to close one's consciousness to alternative interpretations of the phenomenon under discussion before these alternatives have ever been stated"

To participate in this authentic form of mutual address, in this collaborative search for meaning, requires personal courage and analytic ability of a high order. It requires adults to be willing to examine the cultural orgins of many of their beliefs, to be aware of how many of the assumptions that inform their conduct have been acquired from external sources and authorities such as parents, schoolteachers, and peers, and hence to view their dearly held meaning systems as provisional and relative. In this sense to participate in discussion-in the collaborative externalization, exploration, and critical analysis of personally significant meaning systems is to realize one's adulthood to its fullest extent.

Four conditions can be identified that, if they are met, are likely to increase the chance that productive discussion will occur. The first of these is for group members to devise an appropriate moral culture for group discussions. This requires the group to arrive at a set of procedural rules for achieving equity of participation. Second, discussion leaders can give some thought to the materials that are to form the substantive focus of group discullions. The questions to be discussed should not be too factual or too uncontroversial, and they sould not be answerable in the course of preparatory reading by the group. Third, the leader should be well versed both in the subject matter to be covered during the discussion and in the principles of group dynamics. Only someone skilled at dealing with the problems caused by apperent isolates, pressures to silence deviants, and those adults who attempt to use the group as a means of bolstering their self-esteem can be said to be an effective discussion leader. Fourth, discussion participants should be prepared for discussion not only through the generation of a moral culture for discussion session but also through the development of reasoning skills and the improvement of communication abilities. In providing a forum for the pursuit and realization of these reflective analytical akills, as well as in requiring participants to evolve a democratic, moral culture governing group discourse, the discussion method is uniquely suited to facilitating critical adult learning.

Although collaborative discussion is now seen as an effective mode of facilitating learning, the literature that deals with instructional methods is still based mainly on the work of Tyler, and the task of teaching adults is frequently seen as a subcategory of the general task of program devolpment. Teaching is relegated to step three or four in different models of program development, including those of Houle, Knowles, Verner, Lauffer, and Boyle. In fact, teaching is generally not referred to as "teaching" at all, but rather as management of learning experiences, insturctional management, or implecmntation of the instructional plan.

As will be argued further in Chapter Ten, however, this view is only one of a number of approaches to teaching adults. The Tylerian model of objectives-oriented program development in which learners acquire skills and knowledge specified in advance by the teacher and in which success is measured by learners performance of predetermined behaviors is often constraining and overly restrictive. The model does have some utility, but chiefly in the area of psychomotor skill acquisition. Tyler developed his work to assist schoolchildren acquire specific, predetermined skills and knowledge of an unambiguous, technical kind. In some training contexts where it is a question of acquiring technical skills, the sequenced, objectives-oriented nature of the model is highly satisfactory.

The problem is that some facilitators of learning have taken this model as the paradigm suitable for encouraging all kinds of adults learning. Much of the most significant adult learning, however, is of a nontechnical kind. It is concerned with the resolution of moral diffculties, with the development of self-insight, with acquiring the capacity to explore the world views of others, with reflection on experience, and with the evolution of personal ethical codes. One mode of teaching and learning highly suitable for these forms of learning is the discussion method. It is striking just how frequently the educational activities organized by adult learners themselves take this form.

For example, collaborative discussion is

typically found in groups organized by single parents, the recently bereaved, divorcees, homosexuals, newly arrived immigrants, drug abusers, and feminists. These groups are composed of individuals who are seeking a reinforcement of their sense of self-worth. Their members are engaged in a redefinition of self and in a reinterpretation of their past actions and relationships from a newly realized psychological vantage point. They are also all seeking to set forth their experiences, to understand and explore others' experiences, and to heighten their self-awareness through this process of collaborative interpretation. The leadership of such groups is typically rotational. At different times, various individuals within these groups will take the responsibility for encouraging others to contribute to the discussion and will attempt some kind of analysis or interpretation of the experiences that have been voiced.

The adults in these groups are attempting to create new meaning systems. They are reinforcing each others' dormant, half-preceived feeling that there is some massive disjunction between their present ways of living and thinking, on the one hand, and the kind of existence they ideally envisage for themselves, on the other. At times these support and experience exchange groups transform themselves into activist groups that work to change oppressive external conditions. For some groups a common pattern will be a form of praxis in which analysis of common experiences alternates with public advocacy and demonstrations. The very act of participating in a public demonstration in support of gay rights or to demand changes in housing and welfare policies to benefit single parents will serve to strengthen and reinforce these adults' newly adopted and newly created identities. For groups of drug abusers, divorcees, newly arrived immigrants, or the recently bereaved, however, it will often be enough for members to meet regularly for support, for the presentation and analysis of typical problems, and for the gaining of practical assistance in negotiating the changed circumstances of their lives.

Teaching otucomes

We have emphasized that the concept of facilitation should be broadened to include activities in which adults are encouraged to consider alternative ways of thinking and living and in which they are prompted to scrutinize critically the extent to which supposedly universal beliefs, values, and behaviours are in fact culturally constructed. But if we prompt adults to consider these questions, are we not really engaging in a form of amateur psychotherapy? Asking people to reflect on their experience, to consider the motivations underlying their actions, and to try to appreciate the way in which their behaviors are perceived by others sound dangerously close to playing at therapist. This argument deserves to be taken seriously. There are many adults who suffer from clinically diagnosed conditions that range from schizophrenia to severe depression. For an educator to presume to treat them effectively is folly indeed.

There are, however, many adults who are troubled, frustrated with circumstances in their personal or occupational lives, insecure concerning their abilities, and seeking ways to develop more productive relationship with others. Such adults may be disturbed at certain aspects of their personal lives, but they are in no sense clinically "disturbed." There are very few readers of these words, I would venture, who are not disturbed at some aspect of their personal worlds or accupational lives, and it is precisely these adults who frequently form the clientele of adult classes. One of the great tragedies of contemporary life is the overprofessionalization of all aspects of human interaction. We are getting dangerously close to believing that we can engage in thoughtful self-reflection only if we are sanctioned by some professional to whom we pay a fee for the supervision of our self-reflection. Those who accept the argument that adults can undertake reflection on their past actions and current relationship only under the guidance of a skilled psychotherapist are doing nothing more than supporting the professional power and prestige of therapists.

One of the most valuable inquiries into methods of helping adults become critically reflective was intiated by Perry and pursued by Weathersby, Weathersby and Tarule, Boud, and Cameron. Instead of talking in a general wayu about the development in learners of critical awareness and the realization of the contextual, subjective aspects of the world, Perry sets forth nine intellectual stages, which he terms positions. These positions are not meant to be rigidly sequential nor to be mutually contradictory. Additionally, they do not include all the intellectual orientations possible in adulthood since they are derived from a series of intensive interviews with undergraduate students at Harvard. They do provide a useful analytical structure, however, that can be applied to understanding the development of critical reflectivity in adults, without in any way presuming them to be inevitably followed in every case. Indeed, with his undergraduates Perry freely admits that students became frozen at different stages of passive detachment of dualist absolutism.

Put simply, Perry's nine positions represent a move from an initial dualist perspective in which the world is percieved as comprised of black and white, mutually exclusive polarities to onen which the individual has come to a realization of the contextuality and relativity of the world and has then gone on to make a conscious commitment to one of many possible identities. In their exploration of these ideas on ethical growth and intellectual development as they relate to adulthood, the Syracuse Rating Group has also distinguished nine stages in adults' intellectual and ethical development. The final stage of "developing commitments" is distinguished by an awareness of the effect that individual behaviors have on others and by a continuous search for new challenges. This search is undertaken with full knowledge that these challenges involve risks to one's self-esteem and that this final stage is never really "final". In leading up to this final stage, adults typically pass through stages in which they begin to view knowledge as contextual and become able to take on the perspective of others. This recognition of the contingency of knowledge inevitably brings about an appreciation of the socially created nature of knowledge. Immediately prior to stage nine are those stages in which adults realize that only through making a commitment will a sense of individual meaning and responsibility for the creation of their personal worlds emerge.

As Boud has noted with regard to the Perry scheme, "It is helpful for the teacher to have in mind that within the same class there will probably be students with radically different outlooks on what is taking place, who will be reacting in very different ways". An early application of the earlier stages of this framework to a sample of adult students at community college identified dualist, multiplist, and relativist positions among the adults studied. The study noted that faculty in community colleges typically teach content in the same manner, regardless of the intellectual development of class members, and that faculty need to be more flexible in their pedagogic role to take account of the diversity of intellectual stages present in any class.

The Perry scheme ropresents an intersting area of future speculation for theorists of adult learning. Perry's contribution has been to posit an initial framework in which the transition from dualism to relativism to critically aware commitment has been clearly outlined. If these stages can be translated into specific ourcomes, with sufficient flexibility of interpretation so that widely varying settings can be included, this might provide adult teachers with a means by which they could recognize the diversity of stages reached by different members of learning groups. Alternatively, and in a more inductive manner, the frame work provides an analytical construct that one can apply to many different educational initiatives as a way of coming to understand the teaching- learning transactions occuring therein.

There is little doubt that didactic pedagogic procedures in which learners are viewed as receptive repositories eagerly awaiting the deposits of experts are not likely to result in the development of critically aware commitment as outlined by Perry. Rather than looking to concepts of teaching drawn from research on traditional teaching methods, therefore, it might be more fruitful to consult concepts and practices drawn from related fields such as community development or community action. The concept of the animateur is one such ides, and UNESCO has explored the manner in which training schemes to develop animataeurs might be established. At the very least, it is important to realize that between the authoritarian transmission of information to uncritically receptive automata and the nondirective, free-flowing realization of learner-defined activities lies a crucial facilitation role. Facilitators have to be as wary of supporting every inclination, preference, or demand of learners as they are of forcing these same learners to follow a lockstep sequence of previously prescribed educational activities. In both instances learners are liable to develop an uncritical stance toward their own personal and intellectual development; in the one case because their opinion is never challenged or quesitioned, in the other because they are given no choice or chance to voice an opinion. Either option denies the essentially transactional nature of teaching-learning, and both options pretend that challenge, creative confrontation, and self-scrutiny have no place in adult learning. Without these elements, learners may find their educational encounters initially comforting but they will sooner or later come to suspect that such encounters are not really educational at all. When this awareness finally dawns, the resultant withdrawal from participation will have the same significance and result from the same kind of frustration as that caused by the learner's being allowed no voice in the educational transaction.

The global context

Profound changes of various types throughout the world have caused profound thinking regarding the role that education must play in helping people enhance the quality of their lives. Compton and Parish suggest that at least three concerns must be addressed in some way through educational efforts:

1 The increasing gap between the rich and the poor; the gap between rich nations and developing nations.

2 The disproportionate share of the world's resources now allotted to dominant world.

3 The increasing awareness in the Third World of the double standard of living.

Such concerns as these plus the constancy and rapidity of change, suggest to us a need to help people make the most of their individual potential. Boucouvalas describes a standing regulation in Greece that captures this notion of promoting individual ability: "The view of as a self-sufficient and independent personality and as the agent of development". It seems that learner self-direction and self-directed learning skills are crucial to the achievement of this human potential.

The study of self-directed learning appears to be primarily western in orientation and interest, with little relationship many parts of the world. In fact, the majority of recent research, writings, and language related to self-direction in learning have emanated from North America.

We thus believe that it is important to our success with adults as learners to take a more global approach in our understanding about self-direction in learning. We realize that not all our assumptions about learners and their abilities to accept personal responsibility will translate entirely from one setting or culture to another. However, this chapter's purpose is to present some reflections and understandings regarding the universality of self-directed learning principles and approaches.

Some international perspectives on self-direction

We will present some background information before launching into discussions about self-directed learning in selected countries. Both of us have had many international students in our courses. Observing the successes and difficulties involved with facilitating their independent learning have provided us with some understanding of requirements across cultures in applying self-directed learning principles. We also have examined some of the international literature related to self-directed learning and have interviewed and talked informally with several people from other countries to obtain their views regarding such topics as autonomy, learner control, and instructor roles. Thus, what will follow is a summary of the literature we have studied regarding self-direction in selected settings ourside on North America. In addition, for two countries, we present a description of how indigenous adult educators believe that self-direction in learning would be possible in their respective countries.

We also need to say something about the nature of self-direction in learning in various cultures. Based on our reading and conversations with people from various countries, there seem to be many different ideas about what it means to study or plan individually. One country will have as an avowed policy the promotion of individual learning ability, while at the same time advocating participation in governmental sponsored programs to achieve such a goal. Another country will talk about self-education as a primary means for adults to learn, but the nature of the programs described would indicate to a North American observer that rew opportunities exist for individualized decision-making regarding the learning process.

Another problem stems from the structural design of certain approaches intended to promote independent study. For example, a correspondence course that requires strict adherence to a planned route of readings and testing procedure may offer little freedom to the learner other than pacing or sequencing of micro-learning components. Ljosa and Sandvold, on the other hand, make a case for the various ways by which learners can exercise freedom of choice within the didactical structure of correspondence education.

Moore describes how he thought about learner freedom in designing as Open University course. The course was based on: (a) a psychological climate that ecphasized learner decision-making and experience; (b) an emphasis on self-diagnosis; (c) a personally planned route of study; (d) a tutor seen as a resource person; (e) some learner-designed evaluation criteria; and (f) an emphasis on each student's personal learning experiences.

A wide range exists in interpreting and permitting freedoms such as these within the learning setting. As noted earlier in the chapter, some suggest that self-direction is primarily a middle-class, white phenomenon by its emphasis on the individual. Even though some research has demonstated that certain self-directed learning concepts hold across racial, economic, and social groupings, the concepts may not always directly apply in other cultural contexts. However, we firmly believe that as long as cultural context is recognized and respected, it is possible to apply many of the instructional and learning tips described in this book in any setting.

There are many countries that should be examined in terms of their self-directed practices, activities, or philosophies. However, that needs to be the subject of another book as we work toward a better understanding of various implications for the way in which adults are helped in their efforts to maximize their potential. In this section, we touch on just a few countries in order to highlight interesting aspects of self-direction in different cultural contexts.

Scandinavia

Scandinavian countries have a long history of adult education. Grundtvig's pioneering work in Denmark with the folk high school movement began in 1844. Grundtvig, in developing the folk high school movement, wanted an educational experience for adults that was residential in nature but small in scope. He also wanted a mixture of practical and theoretical work, supported by lots of decussion. These institutions therefore stress work in the group setting, and are aimed at the individual development of each person. In fact, their methods and environment are designed to encourage individuals of all social classes to broaden their personal horizons. Folk schools have spread to many other countries in the past century and a half.

Sweden has make several efforts to promote education for adults that is self-directed in nature. One stated adult education aim of the Swedish government, for example, is to cater "to individual preferences and needs" 1977 governmental ordinance called for learning opportunities to increase awareness of personal capacity, to develop independence, to promote creativitym, and to foster critical reflectivity.

One of the most innovative approaches to adult education has been the study circle. These have been used to provide many citizens in Sweden with an opportunity to develop self-study skills.

While the group emphasis of the study circle at first glance may seem inconsistent with notions of self-direction. Oliver states that historically in Sweden: "study circles encouraged self-directed learning and full participation, blending the intensive small group format with traditional Swedish culture-particularly small-town life and the face-to-face conversations of friends and neghbors". Svensson notes that more than 2.5 million people are involved in Swedish study circles each year, with 1.5 million of these women.

While not quite as popular, another important Swedish form of individualized learning is correspondence study. The country has three such organizations: "one that is authorized to hold examinations for formal educational institutions, one that provides study materials that do not lead to any formal qualification, and one that provides agricultural correspondence materials". Nearly 20,000 people each year enroll in correspondence study.

In Norway, correspondence schools have long played a very important role in educating adults. In fact, Norway's Adult Education Act of 1976 was intended to influence learning throughout life and "should give the core ingredient for elf-managed learning throughout the rest of life". Finland, too , has several correspondence institutes that offers expert aid through study centres to assist individual students in their educational efforts.

United Kingdom

The United Kingdom is perhaps most well-known in the area of self-directed education for its pioneering work with the open university concept. There are also many other opportunities for the learner interested in independent study. For example, the number of adults studying by correspondence in the UK is estimated to "range from 500,000 to 750,000 a year".

Another imaginative attempt to foster independent learning took place at Malvern Hills College, the center for adult education in the rural English counties of Hereford and Worcester,

Several adult students were having difficulty attending a regular college class. Thus, a Correspondence Tution Service was established, to "provide individually oriented programmes of home study supported by personal tutorials". An initial diagnostic interview between a tutor and the student, tutorial assistance with learning projects, and home study correspondence courses are some of the avalable resources.

Brookfield also describes his research, which examined the self-directed efforts of individuals not associated with any formal organization or institution. He chose twenty-five working-class individuals whose formal education had ended at age 16, and whose expertise stemmed from extenxive study of, or involvememt with, a hobby or perosnal-interest area. His research helped to advance earlier work, primarly in North America, related to learning projects. It also dedonstrated that independant efforts to obtain mastery over some area of study can take place across a wide rage of cultural and educational backgrounds. He concluded that many adult learners will look to to other learners for information and support rather than to societies, organizations, and professional educators. He noted: "subjects would mention influential books and magazines but would preface these comments by declaringtheir real'source of information was their fellow enthusiasts".

Japan

Japan's progress in industrialization since the Second World War, coupled with its more recent emergence as a world leader in various ways, has prompted a varyety of changes within the country. These range from a growth of pizza parlors and fast-food restaurants, to increasing disposable income for most people, and a constant contact with oither nations. Such changes have also affected education in many ways, including the education of adults. As one example, open-university-type programs reach adults throughout the society.

The pressure to be part of a societal group remains, but subtle changes are taking place in education. A Jaamese, Seiichero Miura, who works sith adult education activities, was interviewed about adult education in his country. He describes the change as follows:

One thing I might mention is the use of groups in adult education practice. I recognize the heavy emphasis in the United States on the self-directed learner. But form looking at human nature I suggest it is not easy for some to be self-directed. In Japan, we would organize a self-directed. In Japan, we would organize a self-directed group, kind of a mixture between group study. Subtle group pressure and a Japanese sensitivity to groups promote a kind of invisible network forcing you to be there, to participate even when you may be reluctant to attend. Thus, you sacrifice your individual desire to the group. I call theis interdependent learning rather than independent learning.

Professor Miura was also asked how he would

introduce learning contracts, frequently used in self-directed learning efforts, into the Japanese culture: "I will introduce the idea of the learning contract but it will be utilized within a group setting. I will need to introduce it slowly and find the ways it can work".

Thus, Japan appears to be in a transitional state where the sanctity of the group is being reevaluated in terms of individual needs and wishes. This may be most clear in adult education effort with older Japanese. Sekiguchi describes a 1981 Recommendation Paper by the Central Committee on Education. Among the Paper's recommendations is a call for the older person's self-education. As a method of study, "learning in a large group or in a classroom will not be adequate since there is a great difference between individual learners. Instead, individual learning methods are recommended as a more suitable way". Facilities such as libraries, museums, and similar institutions are suggested as organizations which need to play a more active role in meeting older adults' needs. Study courses on radio and television and correspondence courses are recommended as effective methods for the older person.

China

The changes that have taken place in China during late 1989 and on into the 1990s make it difficult to comprehend fully what the future holds. However, the last several years have been marked by some important changes relative to adult learning: "Since 1977, when the expansion and restructuring of adult education began after the Cultural Revolution, important changes have taken place in many sectors of adult education". For example, current radio and television delivery methods are patterned after Great Britain's Open University. The Chinese Telivision University opened in 1979 and provides several degree opportunities. In fact, TVUs operate at the national and municipal levels. Telievised instruction is also used at factory colleges, spare-time colleges, and regular universities. Municipal television universities and corresponding study centers in a variety of settings cooperate with centralized programming efforts. They serve some 800,000 registered students and many more casual viewers whdo do not enroll credit.

There are other forms of adult education in China that offer some opportunities for individualized learning. Correspondence courses are avaliable, and individual tutoring is sometimes available. In 1980 factory universities set up correspondence courses that enrolled 240,000 students. Zhou reports that there are some 32,000 people enrolled in independent correspondence colleges, and another 150,000 students enrolled in 148 evening college correspondence divisions.

The "visiting teacher" program also offers opportunities for a leaner to work individually after the teacher provides some initial assistance: "In this program, literacy is taught by a teacher who visits the peasant, with home and labels common household objects the appropriate Chinese characters. The learner thus learns the characters as the items are used"

Indonesia

Traditional beliefs and expectations in Indonesia regarding learning have placed the instructor in a role as authority figure. In fact, learners have not been given many opportunities to assess personal needs as a basis for learning. These learners aslo usually expect the teacher to be an authority on whatever subject matter is being discussed. Furthermore, they view experiential learning activities, such as using various community resources outside the classroom, as a waste of time. They would believe that such time could more appropriately be spent in the classroom listening to an instructor. However, increasing levels of education among the population and a better understanding of teaching approaches outside of Indonesia among educators are indicators that self-direction in learning is possible with appropriate modifications.

For example, one Indonesian educator studying adult education in the United States told one of the authors how he would apply various self-directed learning techniques in introducing family planning to community leaders when he returned home. During his initial contact with the leaders he would discuss the importance for the country of the content to be covered. He would also discuss with them their learning needs, based on their roles, tasks, and functions as community leaders. Because he would be viewed as the authority, he would come well prepared and make the initial presentation with the use of various audio-visual aids.

The participants would then complete a pre-designed, needs-assessment from, and come to some initial conclusions regarding personal needs. This educator would then lead a general discussion to determine needs, strengths, and weaknesses among the group. He would begin by listing learning needs on a chalk board or on poster paper, and ask participants to help him rank them. He would conclude with a summary of the needs, strengths, and weaknesses. Then a description sheet of the content areas that could be covered during subsequent session would be distributed and discussed. He would make every effort to accommodate the uncovered needs, but would be very specific in describing those content areas that he believed must be covered because of official requirements of his own personal convictions, even if they did not match well with the rankings.

After that initial session, he would spend time putting together the plans for remaining sessions. This would include determining who would be responsible for various content areas, what learning aids would be needed, what teaching and learning technique would be used, and what arrangements were needed for outside resources or resource leaders. Passive learning activities would be expected, although small group discussion could be designed for occasional use. If any individualized or experiential learning activities were desired or necessary, special efforts would be needed to make clear the importance of such experiences. As evaluation in the form of testing would be the normal expectation, some efforts would also be needed to design the procedures and instruments.

Thus, some of the self-direction procedures described in this book would be possible, but the instructor or trainer would need to explain such procedures very carefully and help participants understand how they would enhance the learning. Cultural traditions and expectations regarding the role of the instructor do not rule out more individualized approaches, but adaptations based on an understanding of prior expectations of students and teacher roles would be required.

Even the small group discussion typically will center on questions posed by the instructor, although students feel they have some latitude in discussing areas beyond the instructor's question.

Experiential learning activities will be looked at by most learners and instructors as a waste of time. They fear that such activities will take time away from the instructor's lecturing. Although a few learners would thrive probably believe that an instructor using such approaches did not know the probablybelieve that an instructor using such approaches did not know the subject matter and was employing them to cover up for inadequacies. One Tanzanian adult enducator studying in the United States felt that back home his biggest hurdle would be the unwillingness of his university administrators and fellow teachers to accept teaching approaches that placed considerable responsibility on the learner

Another problem area revolves around evaluation and grading. Many of the current traditions of grading were inherited from the British, and the result is usually a highly structured process. For example, many teachers are expected or even required to give a certain number of lower grades. The Tanzanian adult educator mentioned above, who by the time of the interview had considerable experiences with self-directed learning in the classroom from his United States graduate training, felt that the use of a learning contract in his country would be problematic.

The above points suggest that the employment of self-directed learning principles in Tanzania would be difficult, at least initially, because of traditional expectations about education. However, one of the authors spent some time in Tanzania and observed some self-directed adult learning taking place at the village level. In fact, the country supports a national policy of "self-reliance," in which elected village leaders take on primary responsibility for local development.

The policy has worked only coderately well in some parts of the nation and not well at all in others.

Eastern Europe

In most Eastern European countries, a varity of independent study opportunities exist.

Correspondence study seems to be quite popular for the learner who, out of preference of necessity, selects individualized approaches. Albanian workers are encouraged to educate themselves through various forms of education, including correspondence study. Correspondence is also one of the favored delivery methods for adult learning in Bulgaria and Poland.

In Germany, correspondence education is recognized as equal in value to other forms of adult study: "Those who acquire education in this manner are offered special facilities and encouragement, such as leave from work amounting to seventy-seven days per year while retaining the right to a full income". In Hungary, combining both correspondence study and evening courses, according to a 1975 study, "those who acquired a degree in this manner were 45.2% of the total number of people who received a university degree. In Rumania nearly 30 per precent of all adult students study either at evening school or through correspondence.

Yugoslavia is perhaps the most progressive of these countries. It has schools of self-guided learners, developed through federal legislation, and other institutions through which the individual learner uses various enducational resources, such as cultural centres, museus, and liabraries. The country also was among the first nations to provide special study on the conception of andragogy, including both graduate and undergraduate study.

Obviously, the events that have taken place throughout eastern Europe in the dawn of the 1990s will have an impact on the education of adults. While it is too early to speculate with any high degree of confidence, we believe that these changes signals potential for positive developments on the self-direction front. Only time will tell, through, what specific impact may take place.

The issue of wider access is but one of many driving forces putting the impact and process of higher education under scrutiny. The followinng kinds of questions are now the subject of frequent speculation and, more recently, research:

What are students learning and why?

- In what kinds of learning processes are they engaging?
- What is the quality of their experience?
- How effectively and efficiently are resources being deployed to develop tthe potential of new kinds of students?
- What kinds of qualities and competences are being developed and assessed, and for what purposes?
- To what extent do flexibility, openness andd choice obtain with regard to learning struictures and oppertunities?
- Do different kinds of students experience the education offer as 'relevant, useful and enabling'?

> Are students being helped to 'learn how to learn', for a changing world in which social relations are more complex, professional athority and the effectiveneess of traditional structures are being challenged, and knowledge and information increase at a rapid pace?

In this chapter, students, an increasingly influential group of stakeholders but heretofore often invisible in such debates, consider the impact, process and structures of higher education. Their reflections on issues such as quality and responsiveness derive from their experiencee of having returned to academic learning programmes. The voices represented in this chapter come largely from those adults who are often at issuee in access debates. The literature on adults as learners in higher and continuing education tends to reflect the experience of largely white middle-class adults, often North American, who as students or educators have experienced a great deal of previous formal education. In this, they may be similar to other younger adults who have spent most of their school years feeling like this, and who remain under-represented in British higher-education institutions.

The views represented here come from a multi-site qualitative research study. I have investigated the perspectives of adults who have returned to do some kind of higher or continuing education course after an interval of generally at least five years following the end of their initial learning, within and outside formal education, had a bearing on their expectations and experiences of returning to a formal learning context. Through largely individual depth interviews, supported by participant observation and group interviews and discussions, I enquired into meanings about being a learner and learning during the course of these adults' lives in different kinds of situations within and outside formal education.

Broadly, 32 different kinds of learning situations provide the basis from which these adults reflect on their experiences as learners. Overall, 48 learners participated in the study over the course of 8 research cycles, each involving a different formal learning context. Twenty-three of the total 32 who were interviewed individually, and who therefore provided in-depth learning histories, left school with few or no qualification. Only 7 in the study had experienced higher education previously.

Thirty-seven in the study were women: 6 were black. Thirty identified themselves as clearlyy working class, 12 as clearly middle class with 3 unknown. Nine found it difficult to make a distinction, but of this group, felt more working class than middle class.

Six women were followed up, after they completed the diploma at Hillcroft College about which they were first interviewed, and had moved on to university or polytechnic degrree courses. At the end of these second interviews, they had the opportunity to reflect upon the transcript of our previous meeting at which they had anticipated their experiences of higher education.

Disjunction and integration and the return to formal learning contexts: Emergent Themes

Disjunction and the possibility for miseducation

Disjunction refers generally to sense of feeling at odds with oneself, as a learner learning in a particular set of circumstances. It is not the result of a cause-and-effect relationship but rather emerges out of mutually interacting influences, as well as past and present experiences of being a learner in different kinds of learning contexts. A sense of disjunction can be felt to be associateed with who one is, where one is, and how one's present experience as a learner relates to previous or concurrent experiences, within and outside the formal learning context. Disjunction can be associated with feelings of alienation, anger, frustration and confusion. In this study it always refers to a sense of fragmentation and involves issues of both personal and social identity.

Disjunction sets up the potential for education and for miseducation depending upon mitigating circumstances from the past and in the current situation. When miseducation results, thus 'arresting or distorting the growth of further experience', the overall sense of identity as a learner can be fundamentally undermined. Certain kinds of social conditions can lead to the damaging efffects of such an experience becoming internalized.

Alternatively, by chance, design or

conscientious planning on the part of educators, disjunction can be constructively 'made sense of' and managed. This is especially true when various partners in the learning context become more responsible and accountable for what is occuring. This creates the possibility of future actions that can simultaneously compensate for, anticipate and manage disjunction.

There are, however academic learning situations that, by design, intent, or tradition, afford little or no possibility for individual of collective structured reflection on what it means to learn in that situation or on how the situation might be made more effective. The management of disjunction under such circumstances may be more challenging for some learners. The extent to which adults feel able and willing to cope with disjunction, and the concomitant feelings of isolation and lowered self-worth that can be generated, seems to be tied up with many factors. These include the inflences of previous learning and presumptions about education at home and school; experiences of learning and being a learner as an adult within and outside higher education; one's self-concept and overall sense of self-esteem at that time in one's life; the quality of the support and relationships available within and outside the education situation, and the kinds of compensating experiences available at the time in the overall learning environment.

In this study, adults described experiences characterized by a sense of disjunction in relation to the following:

- their expectations of and their initial encounter with the formal learning context;
- the degree of continuity between the new learning experience and prior ones, both within and outside formal education;
- their experience of the assumptions and approaches operating with regard to teaching and learning, and the extent to which these hard with prior expectations and assumptions about learning, based on experience elsewhere;
- the ways in which social differences and power relations were experienced and managed in the learning environment;
- the extent to which core aspects of their personal and social identity felt threatened or at risk in that environment;
- the management of multiple and often conflicting roles;
- the impact of contradictions between tutors'private and public stances; for critical reflection and analysis;
- the ways in which it was expected that knowledge and knowing could be legitimately explored in that learning situation:
- the nature of the dialogue, relationships and learning processes experienced in the formal learning context;
- the ways in whicch personal defelopment and change were occurring:

- in spite of or because of what wass occurring in a particulasr learning situation.

Integration as equilibrium

On the other hand, integration within this conceptual formulation implies that one's sense of personal and social identity does not feel itself to be fundamentally at issue, of at risk, in a particular learning environment. Integration tends to be associated with a sense of equilibrium, or an 'all of a piece feeling'. Integration does not necessarily give rise to learning itself, but rather helps to create the conditions conducive to an individual learner being able and willing to learn in a particular learning situation. In other words, there is potential for benefit, and for education. Integration thus need not be associated with intensely positive feelings.

Integration as hightened self-validation

Integration can also refer to heightened feelings of self-validation, arising out of the extent to which a new situation compensated for prior experiences of disjunction elsewhere. Alternatively, it emerged as a resolution to disjunction involving some kind of invalidation of previously held beliefs, ideas or meanings. It is within this context that disjunction can be experienced as a constructive starting point for learning. The critical difference between the experience of disjunction as an enabling rather than a disabling experience lies in the kinds of values, purposes and relationships which obtain in the learning situation. A critical factor is the nature of the support available to guide the learner through the sense of confusion and fragmentation generated by the experience of disjunction and which enables him, or her to steer a path through it towards significant learning and change. In this study, such situation tended to be characytrized by the adults concerned as feeling valued for who they were as people, and for their prior experience. Learning entailed active involvement and interrelating. Conditions associated with cycles of disjunction and integration, and indeed an overall sense of integration itself in connection with academic learning programmes, included the following: the active used and appreciation of different forms of knowledge, the making of connection across disciplinary boundaries, and a positive valuing and use of personal and social differences within a group. For many learners in this study, to experience learning situations characterized by such conditions and an overall sense of integration, often served to repair severely damaged confidence and self-esteem, and to compensate for prior experiences of education.

Compensating influences

Alternatively, a relationship with a particular tutor could positively mediate an overall sense of disjunction with regard to that course or learning context as whole. Others found that experiences of disjunction on a course could be positively mediated by prior experiences in which confidence had been built, and self-esteem with regard to one's learner identity and potentiality began to develop. Relationship with peers and spouses also played a vital role in enabling learners to make sense of and manage experiences of disjunction. None the less, many of the learners in this study seemed to have required repeated experiences of integration to enable them to feel sufficiently resilient and able to withstane and indeed manage forces which could otherwise damage them. Even then, the path of the development of such resilience and confidence was by no means linear. Certain situations could spiral the learner back into feeling the scars of prior experiences, although in this study no one experienced the feeling of going back to 'square one': earlier experiences that had given rise to a sense of integration had created an internal store upon which to draw when necessary. To survive, and thrive, in academic contexts, however, it seemed that some of these experiences needed to have occurred within formal education.

Imagining: experiencing learning as 'all of a piece'

It would be well beyond the scope of a single chapter to illustrate the many ways in which the concepts of disjunction and integration are grounded in the data. Here, however, I shall draw upon a specific block of material from the study, which was generated in one of two ways. During the course of the initial researh cycles, would often ask participants directly about what they wanted and needed from teachers in higher and continuing education. In later cycles of the study, however, I began to use a role-play approach to get at these needs from another angle. I would ask participants to imagine that just finished my thesis was an expert in a particular subject, and that my first teaching job was with adults such as themselves, many of whom had left school with qualifications and had been away from education for some time. I suggested they advise me as to how I might best approach this challenge, basing their advise me as to how I might best approach this challenge, basing their advice on their own experience as a learner in higher education.

Each of these approaches involved participants in a particular kind of imagining process in relation to their needs and previous expectations. In undertaking it, they teased out the kinds of learning situations and relationships that they saw as conducive to integration and thus to the possibility of education rather than miseducation. The role-play approach, especially, helped to draw out issues which most mattered to these adults if they were to feel willing and able to learn in academic learning situations.

The following main themes emerged from the data elicited by these two techniques: the notion of personal stance in teaching and learning; recognizing and respecting differences; 'unlearning to not speak'; the role of relationship in mediating disjunction; and 'learning-in-relation'. Each of these is dealt with below, illustrating from a particular angle various aspects to the disjunction-integration formulation.

The notion of personal stance in teaching and learning

We often speak about teaching and learning as if

they were simply a function of subject expertise, skill and method. These adults' accounts, however, illustrate the extent to which for them, the quality of teaching, and indeed of learning, is mediated by the 'personal stance' of the teacher. I used this term in the sense of Salmon who suggests that 'the material of learning has traditionally been viewed in different terms from those that define the learner'. For Salmon, the metaphor of personal stance lay emphasis on the personal positions of teachers and learners, and how they give meaning to their learning:

> How we place ourselves, within any learning context, whether formal or informal, is fundamental. This is not just a matter of 'attitude', in so far as it defines our own engagement with the material; it represents the very stuff of learning itself...how we position ourselves towards [each other] in any educational setting... is what governs the limits and possibilities of our engagement together, what shapes and defines the material we construct out of that engagement.

In the accounts which follow, these adults' perceptions and experiences of teachers' personal stances towards them as adult learners are seen as vital to their feeling able to enter into the possibility of education.

For example, Gaynor was a working-class woman in her mid-fifties who returned to do an academic diploma which would enable her to go on to a degree course. She had worked largely inside her home for many years and had little confidence and low self-esteem when she entered Hillcroft College. Speaking within the contexxt of the role-play describeed above, she implores me to remember what it is like to bave no knowledge of that subject at all.

Rhoda, long unejoloyed and with little sense of self-esteem or direction, stresses the negative impact of tutors who position themselves towards their material, rather than towards the student. She is describing here the extent to which she had felt progressively silenced by what she had experienced from certain tutors.

Rhods: They have to be hearing what they have to say. I constantly get interruptions which makes me feel, 'Should I be here?'... And they are always so busy. I always feel I'm taking up his time.

SWW: What about attitudes?

> Rhoda: I always have the feeling with my tutor that he's 'in the know'. He soes most of the talking. He should be more laid back and draw me out more.

Frank was a lower working-class man and previously a labourer who read 12-15 books a week, across at least six subject areas. He re-encountered a former teacher whose previous attempts to encourage him at school had been 'too little too late'. She persuaded him to return as a mature student to an FE college to do O-levels. He did A-levels there also and, after an interval, went on to a polytechnic course. He had, however, condistently encountered structural and attitudinal barriers in his attempts to engage with formal learning contexts. He felt that, during those years of struggle, It was only in political groups that he was able to find the intellectual stimulation and dialogue that he actively craved. Here, he too emphasizes the importance of a personal and social dimension in his interactions with teachers. Unlike many of the women in the above acconts and those that follow, however,, he communicates a certain resilience and autonomy in his expressed wish for confrontation and challenge.

Frank: Their responsibility is to point out the central core of the basic theory, to confront you as an individual. You can then decide if you agree or not ... But they must draw people out. Reach for their potential. Help you to engage with central theory. It is an interactive relationship. This requires knowledge, skills and personal qualities. Also, they must be sensutive to personal problems because these will distort the learning preocess.

SWW: What skills?

Frank: An intellectual grasp. A degree of lucidity with which they can ecplain. Must be evaluated on the extent to which they can facilitate people's interestin and ablity to deal with knowledge and their capacity incorporate within te learning situation the vviews of the students. Especially the older ones. Which may be in direct contradiction and which may not be supported with six million academic references, but practical experience.

Fran was a working-class woman who throughout her initial schooling aimed to be a hairdresser. She eventually became a llecturer and teacherin this field, to the amazement of her family, since they had always seen her sister as the 'academic one' and Fran as the 'practical one'. The ways Fran strived to use her intelligence and creativity in each work situation, however, often seemed to put her at odds with colleagues. One summer, after she had left an unsatisfactory work situation, by chance she came upon information about the local polytechnic's willingness to accept adults without A-levels. She enquired, out of curiosity, and was offered a place. She describes running all the way home, in panic and disbelief. She spent the entire summer trying to persuade officials that, if they were willing to give her a grant to study for three years, they could give her one-third that money to set up her own business as a hairdresser. Failing in this, she began at the local polytechnic in the autumn.

Fran speaks about the need for someone 'with communication skills, and for tutors who can 'break into a language that you can understand.'

> Fran: I could understand what they were saying it would be lovely. They need to talk to me and explain it to me. I would expect them to be positive and encouraging. Usually, if you ask a question, yuo end up with a negative ... They don't use a reinforcing way of learning.

They just sit there and rub up their own ego... One thing they need to know is how to be a teacher. That's the one thing they don't know.

SWW: What does that mean to you?

Fran: If I have so sit and take notes for an hour, which is far too long, I need something that is constructed in a sane pattern. So when I read my notes afterwards, they make sense to me... They ought to be able to use experience, and break into the lecture, without feeling you are taking them off at a tangent... They can't convey what they know...They don't connect it with anybody else's subject matter.

I believe Fran and the others highlight the divide that adults can feel between themselves and their expectations of academic learning situations. Moreover, her own experience as a hairdressing lecturer, after years of apprenticeship and training, led her to feel incredulous that teachers in higher education had preparation only in their subject area.

Recognizing and respecting differences

Adults in the study continually spoke about the importance of being acknowledged and respected for their differences. The interview questions constantly revealed ways in which a failure-in actions, not just words-to recognize and respect their differences could prove a source of disjunction.

Connie was a middle-class woman who had worked entirely inside her home and had taken primary responsibility for parenting. She reached a point where she bought an IQ book, because she felt no better than a 'cabbage'. She returned to higher education via an FE college that catered particularly for mature women returners. This experience had been characterized largely by integration, with continual discovery and challenge emerging out of the quality of the relationships with peers an tutors. She found her transition to the polytechnic unsettling in many ways. Here she emphasizes the effect of different kinds of personal stances of tutors upon her as a learner. In particular, she highlights a confusion she elaborates in other parts of our interview: namely, that tutors are adult learners too, and therefore how can they not understand differences? She speaks sbout the need for tutors to remember that they too are mature students and to use that as a way of relating to mature students. They come with experience. How they see us affects how they interact. They must be helped to see that., 'If you're motivated, you'll get it.' Your pressures are seen as a testing ground. For example, 'You'll be a good rather than realizing the pressures you are under. I wouldn't want the structure and the knowledge to be changed. Just to have more time, and more emphasis on motivation. But sometimes, I just cannot cope. There must be a positive discrimination towards older people.

Todd, a working-class man, had struggled all through initial schooling, feeling out of place in terms of his artists interests. Throughout his education he had felt pressured to be someone he was not, symbolized by the efforts of teachers to turn him from left-handedness to righthandedness. He left school with no qualification and went to work in the markets. Before returnintg to do a degree, he had been both unemployed and a musician, having discovered a relationship with another musician through which he could develop these interests and talents. Here he elaborates on the differences cited by Connie and, like her, stresses the pressures on him in terms of the complexity of his life: in this case, as a musician, as a parent, as one of many in this situation who were not well-heeled financially, and who had anything but the prior learning and life histories of more traditional students. He asserts the need for tutors to recognize

> That we're not just students. We have an outside life too. We suffer the same problems. We're not purely a brain. We're human beings. That's the way it is with normal education. It's not right. But they think they can group us in a lump. Shows a lack of responsibility. Here, they still teach you like you were secondary school. It's the same process: socialize, work, see tutor. But they must know about people like when they are starting to flag. Like this guy who was living in a squat and had to take casual work for four weeks. They have to have skills of working with people: diverse people. People who were delinquent, mentally ill. It's not so much they are misfits. There are lots of really clever people. It's just that they should

> not be treated as if they were academics...No one here has asked me what I am going to do, much less what I have done.

Recognizing differences for a number in the study also meant recognizing previous damage and actively repairing confidence, particulary in the case of women. Sally is another working-class woman who experienced redundancy and separation before her return to study at Hillcroft. Initial education for her had been fraught with one trauma after another. Here she speaks out of her experience of returning to formal education in a women's college where small groups were a key feature of the learning environment. She stresses the importance of recognizing differences in women's pacing and patterning in group dialogue. Once again, the relational aspect of teaching and learning emerges as a central feature:

> I think that is one of the pivots of adult education. Don't have too big a group. They will be overawed. If so, some will be quite vocal. You must use them, take their ideas, but don't let them overawe the others. Encourage those who are quiet. You've got to encourage people to speak, those who are quiet. Don't bully or say, 'What do you think?' I would need time to think about that, but I am sure that there are subtle ways in which you can include people in small group discussion. But the women I know, the women are quite enthusiastic. But the more they get to know you, the more they will open up. I think they are also very afraid of examination

situations and formal learning and they have to be very gently introduced to this.

Unlearning to not speak

Sallly experienced considerable disjunction arising from the contrast between her experiences at Hillcroft, and her university science-based course. In the latter context, she felt an acute sense of fragmentation with regard to the treatment of the discipline, the proces of learning, and the underlying assumption about knowledge and research operating in that environment. Although there was an essential coherence across the latter three, it none the less made Sally feel fundamentally at odds with herself and that environment. The disjunction and subsequent anxiety geneerated by this situation focused her attention on whether and how she could cope, at the expense of academic achievement. Here she describes the other kinds of forces that can diminish or enhance resilience in a learning situation. She reinforces the findings of previous research that women often return to higher or continuing education at a time of trauma or transition in their lives. Here she speaks again about the need to 'repair confidence'. Her conviction indicates how much she too had spiralled back into self-doubt in her new learning situation:

I have realized, being at university, young people nowadays are much more confident, but when women get to my age and are returning to learning, usually and not always, it is for a good reason. They've lost their husband through divorce or ilness, and they have suffered some kind of traumatic experience and need to make a living and they are very very traumatized. In a delicate state. The only way you can describe it is that. And they need not only the ability to learn, but their confidence building. They need to be able to talk about their worries and fears and they need, perhaps, extra time given to them, because they might find it harder to learn after a big gap.

For Sally, integration entails being actively engaged in a learning process which involves actively relating to others, building on their contributions, and gently nurturing confidence. However, she and others often referred to the ways in which they could feel silenced by an intervention, often male—although few conceptualized it in gender terms, and virtually none in feminist terms. But the sense conveyed is that of feeling 'stopped in one's tracks'. Often accounts of such situations awoke memories of being negatively reinforced for being assertive and speaking with conviction. Such forces had taken their toll on women's sense of self-worth and of possibility as a learner.

Karen is a working class woman who had worked largely in secretarial jobs, and had eventually found her way to Hillcroft. She implies how easily tutors can, even unintentionally, abuse their power to the detriment of the learner. Later, at university Karen experienced considerable disjunction in the form of a major writing block on a humanities course. Although the method of teaching was largely in small groups, she felt severely silenced by certain attitudes and stances on the part of some male tutors and later a male counsellor. Here, speaking from the perspective of Hillcroft, before moving into this learning situation, she talks about the need for tutors to approach people, 'on a one-to-one basis, a personal basis, not as teacher-pupil:

> SWW: What would I need to know abouut people?
>
> Karen: To be able to assess personalities. To know who can take harsh criticism and the people who need drawing out more. To know the things that draw them out. Know people's names. That sounds silly, but if you call peoplle by their names, you get this sort of bridge. But the main thing is to treat people as an adult, rather than teacher-pupil... Don't be too harsh in your criticism in certain situations. Not to be patronizing, but put yourself in their position. These women have gone through the same situations as you have. You should approach them on an equal footing, although you are 'imparting the knowledge'. You're sharing it, not dictating it.

Godfrey and Janice also consider the kinds of learning situations that promote their devolopment and learning to fuller potential. For them, issues of personal and social identity, and the experience of differences, are central to the possibilities of education or miseducation. In their learning situation, and in the wider world, the majority group wields a great deal of power and control over opportunity for them and other black people.

Godfrey's description contrasts to some extent with the accounts of the women above, in the sense in which he stresses his autonomy and strength in the face of adversity. None the less, he conveys how a respect for differences and a recognition of the complex social arena within which learning is taking place can be fundamentally at issue for some adult learners. As such he elaborates themes introduced above. Here, in the context of a group interview, he and Janice talk about what they need to feel able and willing to learn. They describe what they experience when they learn with other black people in comparision with how it feels in an acdemic situation, where different kinds of judgement and power are operating, especially when they are in a room full of white people.

Godfrey: When I am challenged and criticized by anyone, I feel every part of me is learning. When cornered, for example, on a platform, giving a speech, I am all angry and aggressive when I'm at my height. If I'm in a group of people and everyone's against me , I learn most. When I must change my self and assimilate what I've learned. Give different interpretations to things. Why, I enjoy people not agreeing with me. Find it beneficial, useful.

SWW: Does it matter who the person is?

Godfrey: I never feel comfortable in a room full

of whites. Never relaxed. Always on guard. Automatic. Immune to it. Unconscious. I speak in a particular manner. More passive in the way I present myself. Not if in a group of black people. More relaxed. It's me! Can curse, do anything. Like when you're angry, revert to your past experience. To learn fully, to be total, must be amongst black people.

Janice: Certainly think you have to be on guard when you are with. Depends on position, authority. Must think of that. Must infringe on you as a person, depending on the group you are in...

Godfrey: I need respect in my environment for me to learn. Plus a stable psychology!

Janice: I feel much more relaxed with a black community group. Because there, constantly raising other people's consciousness.

Godfrey: Also, at these times, when black people challenge you with something. But if they challenge you, that is your view and this is my view. Just leave it. No dreve, no push, no encouragement to continue ongoing dialogue. With group of black people, if someone says, black people are inferior to white, you will argue, say, 'No, no, no.' But in terms of their point of view, will read about it to see where they are coming from. But if white person, will ignore it.

In this account, they engage centrally with dimensions of learning that are at the heart of disjunction and integration. They speak about 'to feel total', 'to learn fully', 'you as a person', 'It's me'. They convey the extent to which a certain sense of integration in their personal and social identity must be felt, in a context of constructive support and challenge. They talk about needing 'a stable psychology' in order to derive maximum benefit from a learning situation. Here they suggest the eXtent to which they have felt it necessary to always be 'on guard' in the learning situation.

Godfrey and Janice experienced a great deal of disjunction of their course, but this was mediated by a number of influences: their opportunities to Reflect on their experIences with other black people, both within and outside that learning situation; their relationship with some signIficant-other peers on their course who could help them to keep in perspective what they were experiencing; theIr determination to get the piece of paper and more power, whereby they could influence the situation of other black people; and finally, the extent to which at the end of their course, tutors began to engage with them in a constructive process of reflection and showed themselves to be valuing actively the perspectives and experiences they bought to the course. Both were involved in advising on issues of process and curriculum, in order to enhance possibilities for education, rather than miseducation.

In these accounts, from those who, not just in terms of age, but also in terms of gender, class and race, have traditionally been under-represented in higher and continuing education, the complexities and struggles in 'unlearning to not speak' become manifest. The possibilities for experience of disjunction, rather than integration, for miseducation, not education, become clearer.

Mediating disjunction

The possibilities for disjunction can be significantly heightened when some of the sources of disjunction remain invisible to, or are actively denied by, tutors. Ethel is another working-class woman who never associated learning with school. She, like many others in the study, found herself on a course at her local polytechnic more as the result of chance rather than design. She experienced considerable disjunction throughout her course, particularly with regard to the emphasis placed on what she regarded as 'knowledge for knowledge's sake' and the extent to which she experienced higher education as an arena where 'they are playing intellectual ping-pong with other people's ideas' rather than creating, originating. Her project work created a kind of oasis for integration, thus playing a significant role in compensating for the disjunction she was experiencing overall: 'My only original work on this course was my research, I loved that.. From June to March I worked non-stop.' A particular tutor also played a key role in enabling her to manage what she was experiencing.

She acknowledges the personal and institutional power that tutors have, and the extent to which this can feel enhanced by the ways in which they choose to use their intelligence. Her account suggests the potentially destructive impact of such power when, for example, the norms of a course, department or institution favour attack and competitive argument as the primary means for 'building people up' intellectually. Alternatively, as in the case of Godfrey or Janice above, such different kinds of power can also combibn with social power, something that was at issue for many on the course - particularly when they were confronted with learning situations where there were few people with whom they could socially identify, amongst their peers of the staff.

Learning in relation

Women's voices predominate in this study, and in their accounts there seem to be fundamental assumptions about learning that can be at odds with the kinds of assumptions about knowledge or teaching and learning that can predominate in academic learning environments. The themes of 'learning in relation' and learning as a process of making connections recur again and again. For many adults in the study, there seemed to be a vital need to make connections: with one's life, with other disciplines, with issues that personally mattered and with experience that was both, prior to and had also emerged out of that course.

For example, Fran talked about how, in her experience, don't connect with anybody else's. For Fran, subject matter is as much 'in her' and in her exas it is in books or in academics' heads. There is nothing in her experience perience that has taught her to discriminate between these forms of knowledge, or to elevate one form above another. To deny the validity of her forms was to deny the validity of her personal and social identity, and her prior experiences of learning particularly outside formal educatiion.

Sally speaks here also from tthe contextgof her university course where as a result of the disjunction she was experiencing she has a heightened sense of the kinds of conditions in which the probability of integration, and therefore of education, is increased:

I think that one of the first things I would say to a student is that everything connects. I had no idea until I came here... So if I were a lecturer here, I would ask others what they were teaching so I could make the connections in my mind and then put it over to the students. Because that is one of the things that amazed me. That no subject is an island. All interconnect and interrelate. And same with the students: they all interconnect and react with each other and need to bounce ideas off each other.

The theme of interweavingg - across ideas, subject boundaries and in the context of one's relationships with peers and tutors - is vivid here.

For many of the women, not to learn in relation, and in ways that enabled them to work from and build upon their existing strengths and understandings, was to put at risk a fragile sense of self-esteem. Those kinds of conditions seemed to nurture trust in one's own voice, without feeling that powerful forces would intervene either to silence that voice, tell it it was wrong , or revive the feeling thattto speak, to write, to create and have access to knowledge in higher education was not really for 'the likes of them'.

Conclusion

Adult learners do not bring their experience with them into education; they are their experience. But the answers to the real complexities and challlenges of this idea do not seem to lie simply in modular programmes, access courses, distance- or open-learning initiatives, experiential learning or andragogy. They lie in much finer nuances of expressing respect, concern and care for individuals, and in giving priority to the need for adults to build upon and make sense of their experiences within the context of their own and others' 'life worlds'.

Issues cruicial to wider access—such as impact and process, boundaries and partnerships and institutional structures—gain in meaning when they are examined from the perspective of learners who, in their bones, can feel the interrelatedness of these dimensions to their experience of learning in higher and continuing education. Moreover, probably better than any of us they can see if and when the Emperor has no clothes.

> People may find it hard to accept that their personal models are not the world as it is but are constructed realities and they are not

soundedly based in absolute truths. When faced with the challenge of, people may be unwilling to accept the responsibility which goes along with the acknowledgement that it is they that construct their own world views. For many, it is more acceptable to believe that their worlds are imposed upon them by the way things really are.

These adults present us with the opportunity to raise fundamental questions about quality and responsiveness from perspectives entirely different from those that usually figure in such debates. For example, to what extent and why do we feel able to assure new kinds of learners of the possibility of education, not miseducation? How do we know if we offer to new kinds of students an education that enables, rather than compounds, previous disabling forces: What more do we need to do and which of our many strengths do we most need to build upon?

In these adults' stories, we find the clues as to the kinds of issues we need to address if we are to ensure that wider access remains concerned with more and different students and quality for all. By reframing the problems, and by exploring alternative solutions, we may very well create new kinds of pathways to enable those of us in higher education to more with integrity and greater clarity through what may now seem only a tangled thicket of demands from too many stakeholders. And in so doing, many other adults may approach our doorways, confident that here we do not just imagine the future, but here the future is lived.

Index